RECORD BREAKERS

Earth and Universe

For a free color catalog describing Gareth Stevens Publishing's list of high-quality books and multimedia programs, call 1-800-542-2595 (USA) or 1-800-461-9120 (Canada). Gareth Stevens Publishing's Fax: (414) 225-0377. See our catalog, too, on the World Wide Web: http://gsinc.com

Library of Congress Cataloging-in-Publication Data

Dunlop, Storm.
    Earth and universe / written by Storm Dunlop.
      p. cm. -- (Record breakers)
    Includes index.
    Summary: Provides information about wind and storms, mountains, earthquakes, and other features on Earth, and similar phenomena throughout the solar system.
    ISBN 0-8368-1948-9 (lib. bdg.)
    1. Astronomy--Juvenile literature. 2. Earth sciences--Juvenile literature. [1. Astronomy--Miscellanea. 2. Earth sciences--Miscellanea.] I. Title. II. Series.
QB46. D86   1997
520--dc21   97-6168

First published in North America in 1997 by
Gareth Stevens Publishing
1555 North RiverCenter Drive, Suite 201
Milwaukee, Wisconsin 53212 USA

First published in 1994 by Watts Books, 96 Leonard Street, London, England, EC2A 4RH. Original © 1994 Orpheus Books Ltd. Illustrations by Sebastian Quigley *(Linden Artists)*, Alessandro Bartolozzi, Luigi Galante *(The McRae Agency)*, Julian Baker, Gary Hincks, Colin Rose, and Roger Stewart. Picture acknowledgements: page 43, Popperfoto Ltd. Created and produced by Nicholas Harris and Joanna Turner, Orpheus Books Ltd. Additional end matter © 1997 Gareth Stevens, Inc.

Printed in the United States of America

1 2 3 4 5 6 7 8 9 01 00 99 98 97

RECORD BREAKERS
Earth and Universe

by Storm Dunlop

Gareth Stevens Publishing
MILWAUKEE

CONTENTS

6 STARS OF NORTHERN & SOUTHERN SKIES
A Guide to Stellar Record Holders
· The Brightest Stars

8 THE LARGEST VISIBLE STAR
Betelgeuse, the Size of 800 Suns · The Life and Death of a Star · The Largest Stars · The Smallest Stars

10 BLACK HOLES
The Densest Objects in the Universe · Massive Energy Machines

12 THE NEAREST STAR
A Shimmering Ball of Gas
· Daytime Darkness

14 THE PLANETS
Solar System Record Holders · The Inner Planets · The Outer Planets

16 TO THE CENTER OF JUPITER
Giant Among Planets · The Great Red Spot

18 THE HOTTEST PLANET
Beneath the Sulfurous Clouds of Venus · Meteoroid Bombardment

20 OLYMPUS MONS
The Highest Mountain in the Solar System · The Red Planet

22 THE LARGEST MOONS
Worlds of Ice and Rock · The Smallest Moon

24 HALLEY'S COMET
The Brightest Short-Period Comet
· A Cometary Journey
· What is a Comet?

26 EARTH RECORD HOLDERS
Our Home Planet · The Largest Lakes · The Longest Rivers · The Largest Islands

28 THE GREATEST OCEAN
The Mighty Pacific · Beneath the Ring of Fire

30 THE GREATEST MOUNTAIN RANGE
The Mid-Oceanic Ridge · Volcanoes under the Sea

32 THE HIGHEST MOUNTAINS
The Towering Himalayas
· Colliding Plates · The World's Highest Mountains

34 THE GREATEST RIFT
And the Longest River · The Nile
· East Africa Splits Apart

36 THE LARGEST GORGE
The Spectacular Grand Canyon
· History in the Rocks

38 THE DEEPEST LAKE
Baikal, Blue Eye of Siberia · A Giant Chasm · A Climate of Its Own

40 THE GREATEST EXPLOSION
A Volcano Blows · Under a Volcano
· Famous Volcanic Eruptions of the Past

42 THE GREATEST EARTHQUAKE
The Great Chilean Quake · Giant Waves · Some Giant Earthquakes

44 THE MOST POWERFUL STORM
The Deadly Tornado
· The Tri-State Twister

46 GLOSSARY · RESEARCH PROJECTS · BOOKS · VIDEOS · WEB SITES · PLACES TO VISIT

48 INDEX

INTRODUCTION

IMAGINE A STAR SO GIGANTIC that, even if you traveled in the fastest plane, it would take over five hundred years to fly around it. In addition, there are regions in space, called black holes, so tiny they are smaller than the ball of a ballpoint pen. And even though some black holes are incredibly distant, astronomers can still detect where these objects are. Likewise, our own **Solar System** contains many astonishing record holders. Tornadoes on Earth are extremely destructive, but winds on Saturn are more than ten times as fast. The swirling storm of the Great Red Spot on Jupiter is twice the size of Earth itself. Some sunspots can be more than twenty times as large as Earth. Venus is so hot that any astronaut who landed there would be immediately incinerated. Pluto is so cold — below -328° Fahrenheit (-200° Celsius) — its surface is made of frozen gases.

How does Earth's Grand Canyon compare with the giant valleys on Mars? Where is the world's deepest lake, its highest mountain, and its longest river? When and where did the world's most powerful earthquake occur? Find the record-breaking answers to these and many more questions in this book.

Words that appear in the glossary are in **boldface** type the first time they occur in the text.

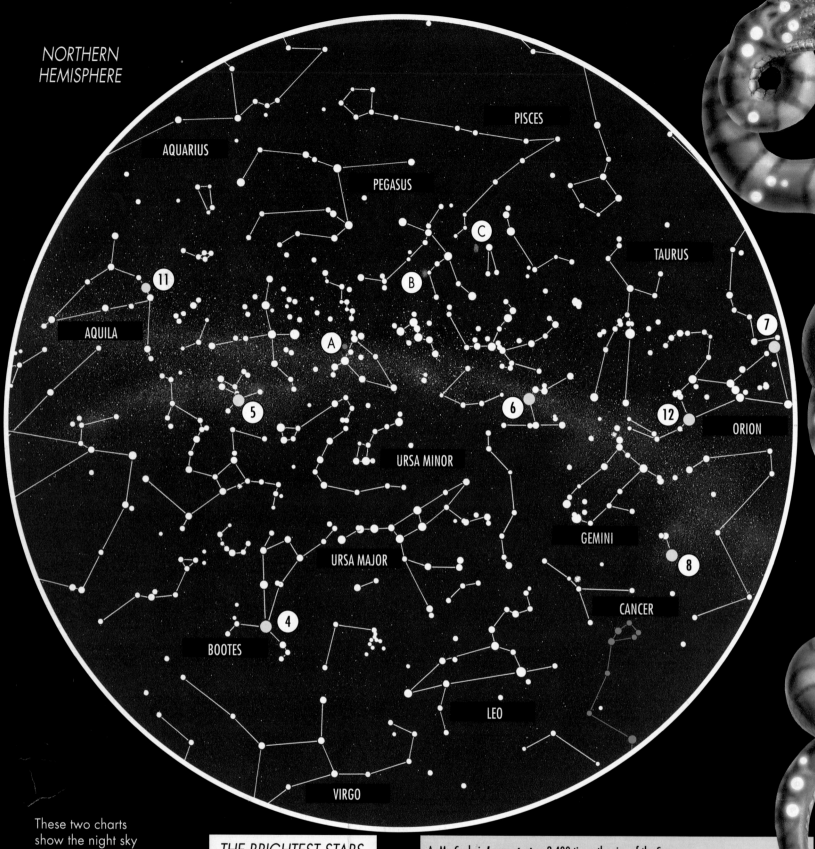

AQUARIUS

PISCES

PEGASUS

TAURUS

11

AQUILA

A

B

C

7

5

6

12

ORION

URSA MINOR

GEMINI

8

URSA MAJOR

CANCER

4

BOOTES

LEO

VIRGO

These two charts
show the night sky
visible from the
Northern Hemisphere
(left) and Southern
Hemisphere *(right)*.
Over the course of
a year, the part that
is visible varies.
The brighter stars
are shown as larger
spots. The lines
between the stars link
those stars together
in a **constellation**.

THE BRIGHTEST STARS

1 Sirius
2 Canopus
3 Alpha Centauri (Rigil Kent)
4 Arcturus
5 Vega
6 Capella
7 Rigel
8 Procyon
9 Achernar
10 Hadar
11 Altair
12 Betelgeuse

A Mu Cephei **Largest star** 2,400 times the size of the Sun
B M31 galaxy **Farthest object easily visible to the eye**
   2.5 million light-years away
C M33 galaxy **Farthest object ever visible to the eye** 2.6 million light-years away
D Sirius **Brightest star** 8.6 light-years away
E Hydra **Largest constellation**
F Large Magellanic Cloud **Second nearest galaxy** 169,000 light-years away
G Eta Carinae **Most massive star** 200 times the mass of the Sun
H Crux **Smallest constellation**
J Proxima Centauri **Nearest star** 4.2 light-years away
K Alpha Centauri (Rigil Kent) **Second nearest star and nearest visible to the eye**
   4.4 light-years away
L Sagittarius Dwarf Galaxy **Nearest galaxy** 50,000 light-years away

STARS OF NORTHERN & SOUTHERN SKIES
A GUIDE TO STELLAR RECORD HOLDERS

IMAGINE FLYING in the Concorde at its cruising speed of 1,450 miles (2,333 kilometers) per hour. It would still take nearly 200,000 years to reach the nearest star! Distances in the universe are so vast that scientists use a special measurement called a **light-year**. Light moves at 186,290 miles (299,792 km) per second. (In comparison, it would take the Concorde nearly five-and-a-

half days to cover the same distance.) A light-year is the distance light travels in a year. Scientists use this unit to measure distances in outer space instead of dealing in millions and millions of miles or kilometers. The farthest known objects in space are **quasars**. They are the central regions of **galaxies**. They throw out enormous amounts of light and heat.

PISCES

CETUS

AQUARIUS

CAPRICORNUS

11

L

9

F

7

ORION

12

D 1

CANIS MAJOR

2

J

10 3 K

H

G

8

CENTAURUS

LIBRA

E

The largest constellation is called Hydra. It was named after a mythical sea monster *(above)*. Hydra contains about 68 stars visible to the eye *(not all shown)* and covers 3 per cent of the entire sky.

VIRGO

SOUTHERN HEMISPHERE

THE LARGEST VISIBLE STAR
BETELGEUSE, THE SIZE OF 800 SUNS

THE LARGEST STARS	
Mu Cephei	2,400
VV Cephei B	1,600
Antares	1,000
Betelgeuse	800
Ras Algethi	600
(times the size of the Sun)	

THEY MAY LOOK like only tiny points of light in the night sky, but stars can be enormous — sometimes millions of times the size of Earth. The very largest stars are called supergiants. Of all the stars that can be seen *with just the naked eye*, Betelgeuse is the largest. It is the bright red star in the constellation Orion. About 691 million miles (1.112 billion km) across, it is 800 times the size of the Sun.

It is very difficult to measure the sizes of stars because they are so far away. Astronomers do not always agree which is the largest star of all. It is probably Mu Cephei, a star about 2,400 times the size of the Sun.

One way to imagine the size of supergiant stars is to compare them with the orbits of planets in our Solar System *(below)*. Betelgeuse would engulf Mercury, Venus, Earth, and Mars — all the inner planets circling the Sun. The supergiant Mu Cephei would consume Jupiter and Saturn, as well.

THE LIFE AND DEATH OF A STAR

Stars are formed when clouds of gas and dust in space (1) shrink and become dense blobs called protostars (2). Gravity causes the shrinking. The core of the new protostar becomes so hot that nuclear reactions *(see page 12)* start deep inside it. Gas and dust are blown away by a violent wind from the star (3). Sometimes a spinning disk of dust, gas, and ice results (4). This may eventually become the birthplace of planets. The fuel that powers the nuclear reactions lasts billions of years (5).

THE SMALLEST STARS

Stars like the Sun are so small when compared with giant and supergiant stars that astronomers call the smaller stars dwarfs. A teaspoonful of material from the Sun is as heavy as a teaspoonful of syrup. After the Sun swells to become a red giant (in about five billion years), it will lose its outer layers. Just the small, very hot, dead core will remain. Called a white dwarf, it will then measure about 6,214 miles (10,000 km) across (roughly the size of Earth) and be extremely dense. A teaspoonful of white-dwarf material weighs 5.5 tons (5 metric tons).

The core that remains after a supernova explosion is a tiny star no more than 16 miles (25 km) across. It is a neutron star, the smallest type of star that exists. A teaspoonful weighs 1.1 billion tons (1 billion metric tons)!

Compared to other types of stars, neutron stars are very small. A neutron star is contrasted with a view of New York City *(above)*.

When it runs out, the core collapses, and the outer regions grow into red giants (6). Most stars, including our Sun, are destined to become red giants. Some much heavier stars become supergiants (7).

When its nuclear fuel runs out, a supergiant's core collapses in a split-second. The outside explodes as a supernova, the greatest explosion known in all of nature (8). For a fraction of a second, a supernova will give off more energy than all the billions of stars — in every one of the billions of galaxies — all put together! All that is left after the explosion is a dense neutron star (9) or a **black hole** *(see pages 10-11)*.

BLACK HOLES
THE DENSEST OBJECTS IN THE UNIVERSE

Bneutron stars *(see page 9)*, they are all that remains of stars that have exploded into supernovas.

All objects in space have a force of gravity. It is this force that holds stars together, keeps the planets in their orbits around the Sun, and causes all objects on Earth to fall to the ground. To escape from a star or planet, you would have to travel at very high speeds to overcome the force of gravity. A rocket launched from Earth must go faster than 25,055 miles (40,320 km) an hour to escape from Earth's gravitational pull.

After a supernova explosion, the central core collapses until it is a tiny fraction of the size it once was. Just a pinpoint in space, it is surrounded by a

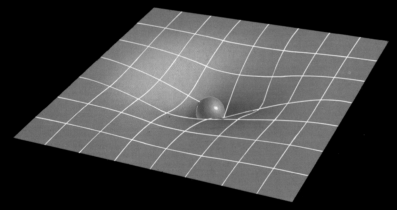

Think of the force of gravity as a ball on a rubber sheet. Stars and planets "bend" space in this manner. Anything close by will fall toward them. If the ball got so heavy that part of the sheet stretched into a long, thin tube, it would become a black hole.

An enormous, swirling disk of gas surrounds a giant black hole in the center of a quasar. The incredible energy blasts two jets of gas into space.

force of gravity more powerful than any normal star in the Universe. To escape from this area, you would have to travel faster than the speed of light — 186,290 miles (299,792 km) per second! In fact, escape would be impossible because nothing can travel faster than the speed of light. These mysterious, invisible objects are called black holes. Nothing, not even light, can escape them.

No one has ever seen a black hole, but astronomers have determined they exist because powerful gravitational forces from them can be detected.

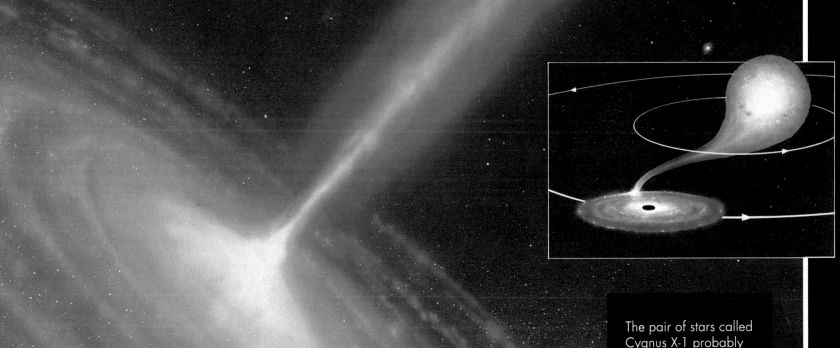

The pair of stars called Cygnus X-1 probably contains a black hole. A supergiant star *(above)* circles something invisible that has an enormous gravitational pull. The star is losing gas, which swirls down into the black hole.

MASSIVE ENERGY MACHINES

Astronomers think black holes lurk in the centers of galaxies. In some galaxies, such as our own Milky Way, the black holes are fairly peaceful. In others, there is violent activity. Quasars, the most distant objects in the Universe, are probably the central regions of such violent galaxies. The energy quasars give out is so great it can be detected even though the galaxies themselves are too far away to be visible.

THE NEAREST STAR
A SHIMMERING BALL OF GAS

THE NEAREST STAR to Earth is the Sun itself. A gigantic ball of extremely hot gases, mostly hydrogen and helium, the Sun is big enough to contain nearly 1,400,000 bodies the size of Earth. It dwarfs even the largest planet, Jupiter. In fact, the Sun contains more than 99 percent of all the matter in our Solar System. The Sun also provides most of the heat in the Solar System — the warmth that makes life possible on Earth.

The Sun's surface, called the **photosphere**, is in constant motion, like water boiling in a kettle. Its temperature is about 10,832°F (6,000°C). At the center, the temperature rises to an incredible 59 million°F (15 million°C). The core generates all the Sun's energy through what are known as nuclear reactions. At such high temperatures, hydrogen is changed into helium in a reaction that gives off an enormous amount of energy. This is called **nuclear fusion**.

Scientists have created temperatures far hotter than at the center of the Sun. At a facility in southern England called the Joint European Torus laboratory, temperatures at the center of controlled nuclear fusion experiments are about 752 million°F (400 million°C).

The Sun burns about 4.4 million tons (4 million metric tons) of hydrogen every second. But our Sun is so enormous that, fortunately for us, it will take another five billion years before it exhausts itself.

Prominences *(above)* are the clouds, tongues, or arches of glowing gas held above the Sun by magnetic fields. Some prominences last for weeks, but other more violent ones last only hours. Many prominences are gigantic. The highest arches are often more than 372,840 miles (600,000 km) high, twice the distance from Earth to the Moon.

Sudden explosions of energy on the Sun's surface are called flares. The strongest flares release in a few minutes as much energy as the entire Sun does in a few seconds. One of the greatest solar flares of recent times happened on August 10, 1989. It blacked out the power supply in Quebec, Canada.

Sunspots

In this illustration of the Sun, a segment has been removed so that the layers inside are visible.

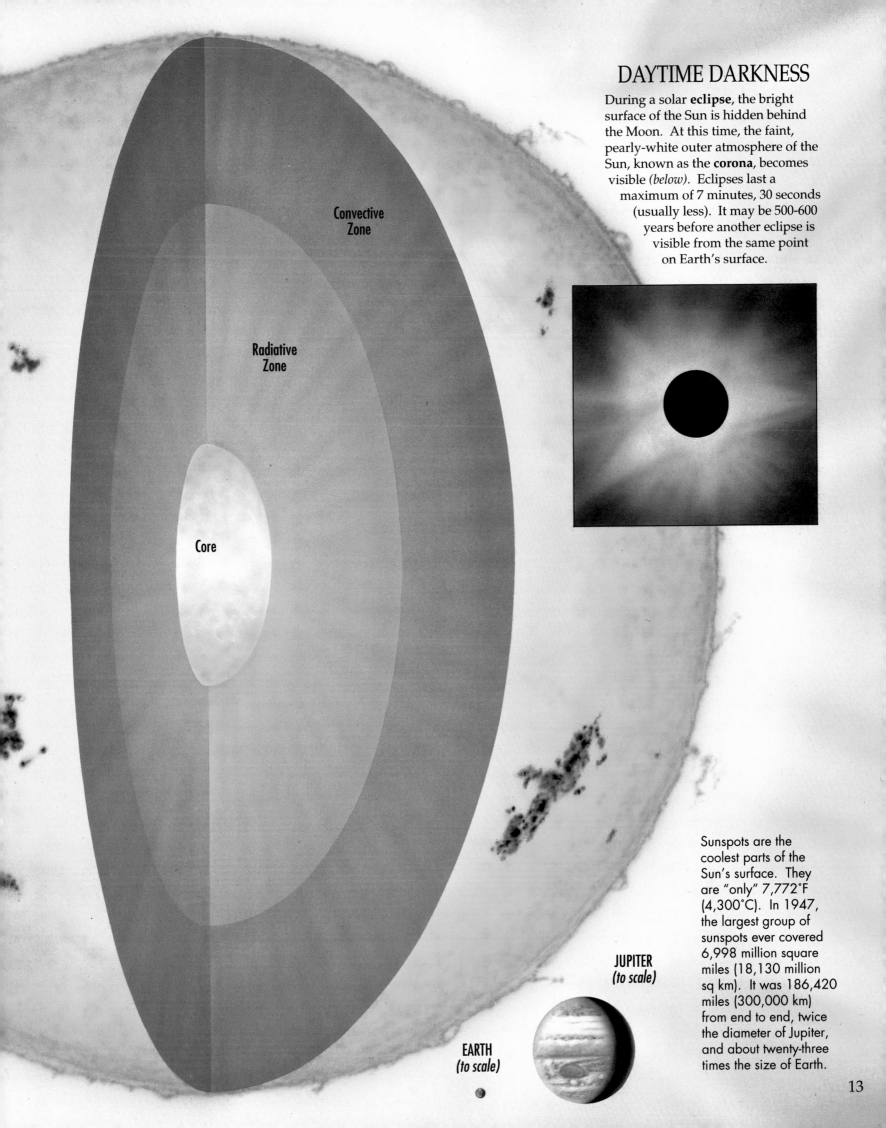

Convective Zone

Radiative Zone

Core

DAYTIME DARKNESS

During a solar **eclipse**, the bright surface of the Sun is hidden behind the Moon. At this time, the faint, pearly-white outer atmosphere of the Sun, known as the **corona**, becomes visible *(below)*. Eclipses last a maximum of 7 minutes, 30 seconds (usually less). It may be 500-600 years before another eclipse is visible from the same point on Earth's surface.

Sunspots are the coolest parts of the Sun's surface. They are "only" 7,772°F (4,300°C). In 1947, the largest group of sunspots ever covered 6,998 million square miles (18,130 million sq km). It was 186,420 miles (300,000 km) from end to end, twice the diameter of Jupiter, and about twenty-three times the size of Earth.

JUPITER
(to scale)

EARTH
(to scale)

13

Bare, rocky Mercury is the planet closest to the Sun. It has the smallest orbit around the Sun — circling it in eighty-eight days.

The hottest planet, Venus, spins slowly, so it has the longest day. It comes closer to Earth than any other planet.

MERCURY

VENUS

EARTH

MARS

THE INNER PLANETS

MERCURY *Diameter* 3,031 miles (4,878 km); no moons; bare, rocky surface.

VENUS *Diameter* 7,521 miles (12,104 km); no moons; hot, cloud-covered.

EARTH *Diameter* 7,927 miles (12,756 km); 1 moon; extensive oceans.

MARS *Diameter* 4,222 miles (6,794 km); 2 moons; dry, dusty surface, with little **atmosphere**.

Mars is a very cold and dry planet. It has the highest mountain in the Solar System.

Jupiter is larger than all the other planets combined. It spins the fastest and has the shortest day of all.

SUN

JUPITER

Mercury Venus Earth Mars   Asteroids   Jupiter   Saturn   Uranus

THE PLANETS
SOLAR SYSTEM RECORD HOLDERS

Saturn has the most moons (18) and the largest rings. It has the lowest density — even less than that of water.

SATURN

THE LARGEST PLANETS in our Solar System — Jupiter, Saturn, Uranus, and Neptune — are known as the gas giants. Unlike our rocky planet Earth, these planets consist mostly of gases, particularly hydrogen and helium. Jupiter and Saturn probably have rocky cores, but the others may have only liquid water and methane beneath their gassy exteriors.

The gas giants all have many moons, some of which are larger than Mercury or Pluto, the two smallest planets. The giant planets also all have rings, although except for Saturn's, they are very faint. Saturn's bright rings consist of millions of blocks of ice, the largest of which are about 33 feet (10 meters) across.

The outermost and smallest planet, Pluto is mostly made of ice. Its orbit around the Sun is more elongated than those of the other planets. This means, some of the time, it is actually closer to the Sun than Neptune.

The four small, inner planets — Mercury, Venus, Earth, and Mars — are made mainly of rock. Between Mars and Jupiter, thousands of asteroids (also called minor planets) orbit the Sun. The largest, Ceres, is 623 miles (1,003 km) across.

The Sun and planets are illustrated to scale.

Uranus was the first planet to be discovered through the use of a telescope.

URANUS

Neptune is the farthest planet studied by any space probe.

THE OUTER PLANETS

JUPITER *Diameter* 88,736 miles (142,800 km); 16 moons; tiny ring.

SATURN *Diameter* 74,568 miles (120,000 km); 18 moons; giant rings.

URANUS *Diameter* 32,313 miles (52,000 km); 15 moons; 10 rings.

NEPTUNE *Diameter* 30,076 miles (48,400 km); 15 moons; 2 rings.

PLUTO *Diameter* 1,429 miles (2,300 km); 1 moon.

NEPTUNE

Pluto, the most distant planet from the Sun, has a single moon, Charon. It is also the smallest and coldest planet.

PLUTO

Pluto   Neptune
(when nearest the Sun)

This diagram shows the planets' relative distances from the Sun.

Pluto

TO THE CENTER OF JUPITER
GIANT AMONG PLANETS

WITH A DIAMETER more than eleven times that of Earth, Jupiter is the largest of all the planets in our Solar System. Jupiter could contain a thousand Earths! Its gravity is so strong that it often alters the orbits of comets that pass closely by (see pages 24-25), sometimes hurling them out of the Solar System.

Jupiter's day is shorter than that of any other planet — just under ten hours. Because it rotates so fast, Jupiter bulges at its equator and measures 5,344 miles (8,600 km) less from pole to pole. Jupiter has no solid surface. Only its core (with a diameter more than twice that of the entire Earth) is made of rock and metals. Most of the globe is liquid — not water, but a metallic form of hydrogen close to the core; and liquid hydrogen beneath the clouds near its surface.

Like the other outer planets — Saturn, Uranus, and Neptune — Jupiter is surrounded by swirling clouds of gas. Divided into bright zones and dark belts, Jupiter's clouds are separated by bands of high-speed winds. Some reach speeds of 336 miles (540 km) per hour. Saturn holds the record, however, with winds up to 1,119 miles (1,800 km) per hour — faster than the speed of sound on Earth!

Fast-moving clouds that circle Jupiter are constantly changing shape. A faint, dusty ring, probably only a few miles (km) thick, also surrounds the planet. Jupiter's most famous feature is, however, the Great Red Spot (in red box), shown in greater detail on the opposite page.

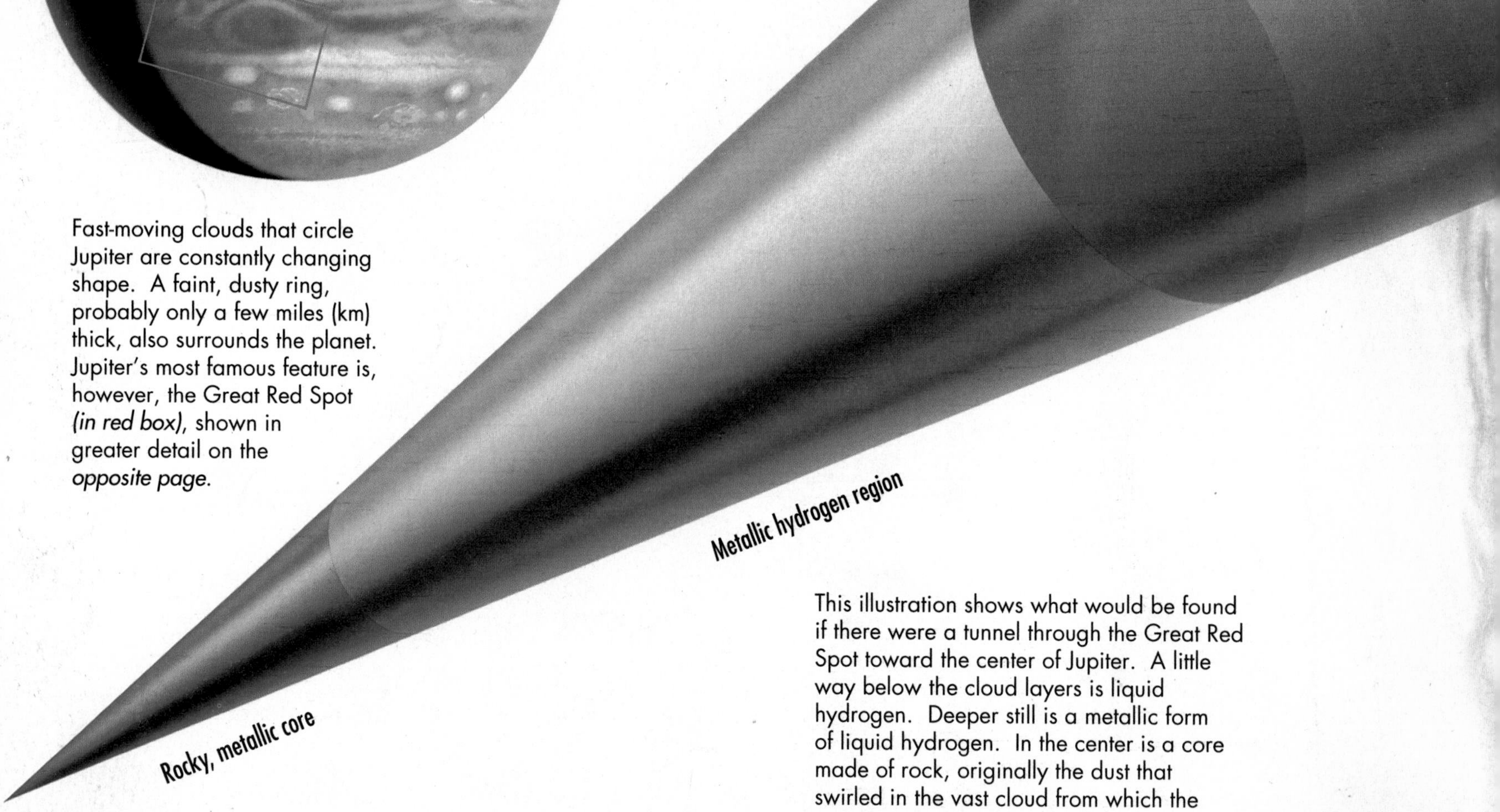

Metallic hydrogen region

Rocky, metallic core

This illustration shows what would be found if there were a tunnel through the Great Red Spot toward the center of Jupiter. A little way below the cloud layers is liquid hydrogen. Deeper still is a metallic form of liquid hydrogen. In the center is a core made of rock, originally the dust that swirled in the vast cloud from which the Sun and planets were born (see pages 8-9).

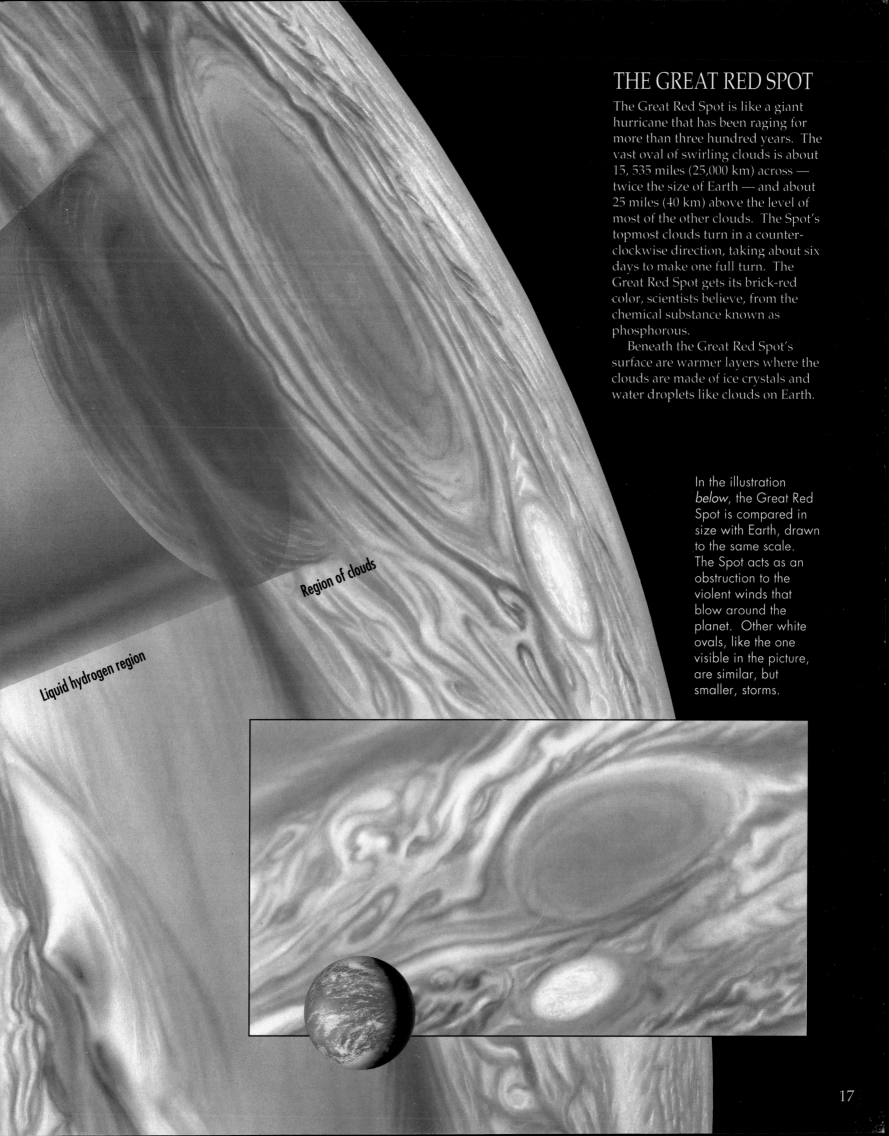

THE GREAT RED SPOT

The Great Red Spot is like a giant hurricane that has been raging for more than three hundred years. The vast oval of swirling clouds is about 15, 535 miles (25,000 km) across — twice the size of Earth — and about 25 miles (40 km) above the level of most of the other clouds. The Spot's topmost clouds turn in a counter-clockwise direction, taking about six days to make one full turn. The Great Red Spot gets its brick-red color, scientists believe, from the chemical substance known as phosphorous.

Beneath the Great Red Spot's surface are warmer layers where the clouds are made of ice crystals and water droplets like clouds on Earth.

In the illustration *below*, the Great Red Spot is compared in size with Earth, drawn to the same scale. The Spot acts as an obstruction to the violent winds that blow around the planet. Other white ovals, like the one visible in the picture, are similar, but smaller, storms.

Region of clouds

Liquid hydrogen region

THE HOTTEST PLANET
BENEATH THE SULFUROUS CLOUDS OF VENUS

VENUS IS THE NEAREST PLANET to Earth, but no world could be an unfriendlier place to visit! Venus is the hottest planet in the Solar System. Its average temperature of 914°F (490°C) can easily melt lead. It is even hotter than Mercury, although that planet is much closer to the Sun. This is because Venus's thick atmosphere of carbon dioxide prevents heat from escaping.

Most of the barren surface is covered by vast plains, studded with tens of thousands of volcanoes. The mountain known as Maxwell Montes is nearly 7.5 miles (12,000 m) high. It is the second highest mountain in the Solar System after Olympus Mons *(see pages 20-21)* on Mars.

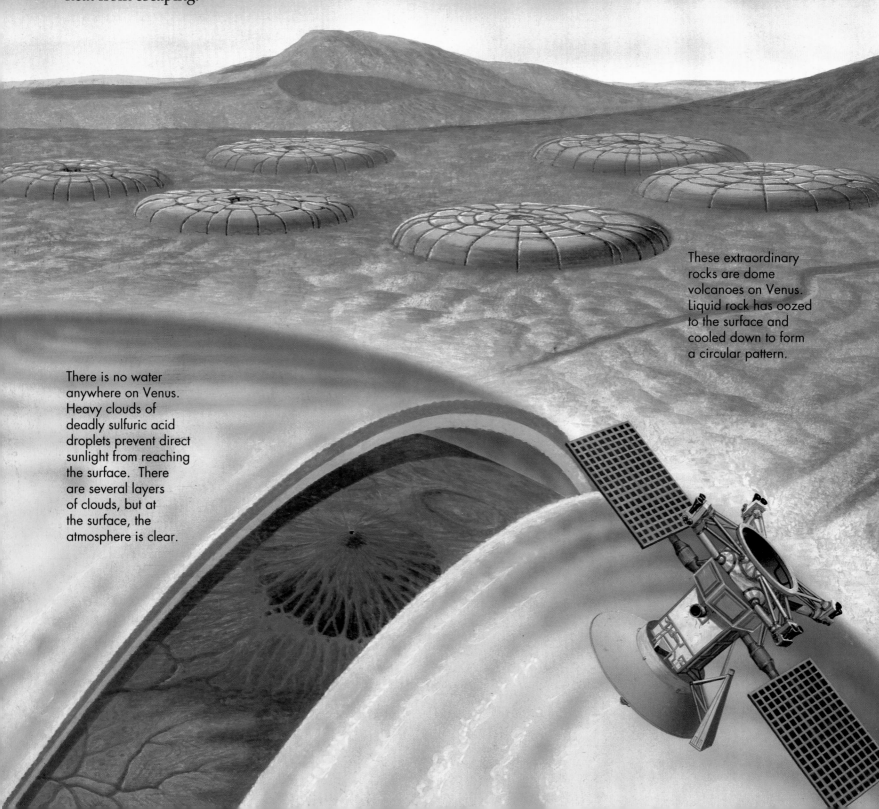

These extraordinary rocks are dome volcanoes on Venus. Liquid rock has oozed to the surface and cooled down to form a circular pattern.

There is no water anywhere on Venus. Heavy clouds of deadly sulfuric acid droplets prevent direct sunlight from reaching the surface. There are several layers of clouds, but at the surface, the atmosphere is clear.

METEOROID BOMBARDMENT

A **meteoroid** is a fragment of rock and ice shooting around the Solar System. Many are completely destroyed in the dense atmosphere of Venus before they get near the surface of the planet. Some explode in mid-air. The shock wave from the explosion shatters the rocks on the surface below. The largest meteors smash to the ground with tremendous force, flinging rocks in all directions. The largest craters are about 68 miles (110 km) across.

Modern technology has revealed what Venus really looks like. A spacecraft called *Magellan (left)* has mapped the planet's surface beneath the clouds. To accomplish this, it used **radar**, the same device ships and airplanes use to detect other craft out of direct vision.

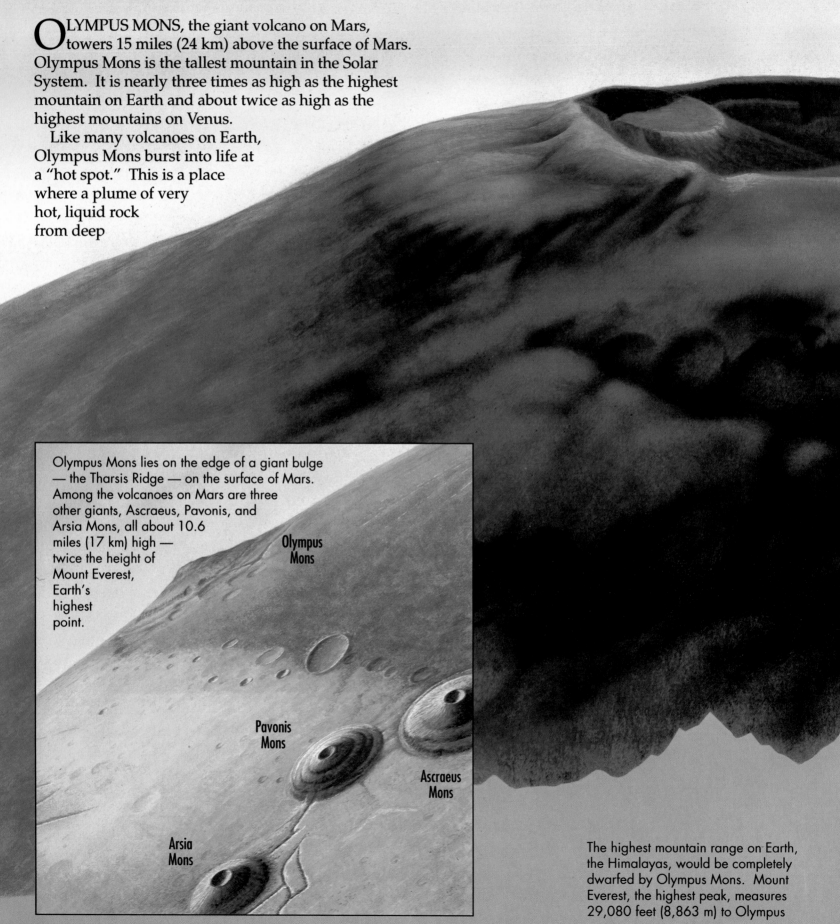

OLYMPUS MONS
THE HIGHEST MOUNTAIN IN THE SOLAR SYSTEM

OLYMPUS MONS, the giant volcano on Mars, towers 15 miles (24 km) above the surface of Mars. Olympus Mons is the tallest mountain in the Solar System. It is nearly three times as high as the highest mountain on Earth and about twice as high as the highest mountains on Venus.

Like many volcanoes on Earth, Olympus Mons burst into life at a "hot spot." This is a place where a plume of very hot, liquid rock from deep

Olympus Mons lies on the edge of a giant bulge — the Tharsis Ridge — on the surface of Mars. Among the volcanoes on Mars are three other giants, Ascraeus, Pavonis, and Arsia Mons, all about 10.6 miles (17 km) high — twice the height of Mount Everest, Earth's highest point.

Olympus Mons

Pavonis Mons

Ascraeus Mons

Arsia Mons

The highest mountain range on Earth, the Himalayas, would be completely dwarfed by Olympus Mons. Mount Everest, the highest peak, measures 29,080 feet (8,863 m) to Olympus

below the surface of a planet melts through its outer crust. Earth's outer crust is constantly on the move, a fractured armor of plates sliding against, alongside, or beneath each other *(see page 32)*. Hot-spot volcanoes, such as the Hawaiian Islands in the Pacific Ocean, appear at the surface of Earth in different places as a plate wanders over a molten spot.

Unlike the Hawaiian volcanoes, Olympus Mons stayed put above its hot spot. The eruptions and **lava** flows have gone on for tens — perhaps hundreds — of millions of years. As each layer of rock cooled, the volcano grew larger and larger. It now measures about 373 miles (600 km) across.

Area of inset
(opposite page)

THE RED PLANET

Mars is the red planet. Its color comes from substances containing iron in its surface rocks. Nearly 50 million miles (80 million km) farther from the Sun than Earth, Mars is a cold world. Sometimes the temperature reaches the melting point of water 32°F (0°C) at the equator in summer. In winter, it plunges to below -184°F (-120°C) over the poles, which are capped by layers of frozen carbon dioxide and ice made of water. In the north, an expanse of ice remains frozen in the summer. It is surrounded by the largest area of sand dunes known in the Solar System, stretching nearly around the planet.

Now Mars is a dry and dusty place, but water once flowed over its surface. Dried-up riverbeds are all that remain. Vallis Marineris is a gigantic **rift valley** *(see pages 34-35)* on Mars. It is about 2,486 miles (4,000 km) long, nearly enough to reach from coast to coast of the United States. Parts of it are about 3.73 miles (6 km) deep, nearly four times as deep as Earth's greatest gorge, the Grand Canyon *(see pages 36-37)*.

Mons's 86,618 feet (26,400 m)! And just five mountains the size of Olympus Mons placed side by side would be roughly as long as the entire Himalaya range *(see pages 32-33)*.

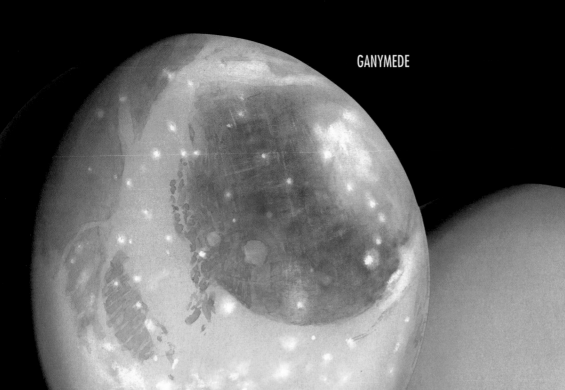

GANYMEDE

Saturn's moon, Titan, 3,200 miles (5,150 km) across, is one of the few moons in the Solar System with an atmosphere. Thick clouds permanently hide the icy surface from the Sun, while methane rains fall in an everlasting shower.

TITAN

Jupiter's four largest moons are all in the top seven. They are called the Galilean satellites after the Italian scientist Galileo, who first discovered them in 1610. Ganymede, the largest of all, is 3,279 miles (5,276 km) across. It has an icy surface, with dark plains. It contains areas showing a grooved pattern, as if the surface had been clawed away by a giant fork.

THE SMALLEST MOON

The smallest moon (excluding smaller fragments of rock and ice circling the larger planets) is Deimos. It completes its orbit around Mars every 30 hours, 20 minutes. Shaped like a giant potato, it is about 9.3 miles (15 km) long, roughly three-quarters the length of Manhattan Island (New York) *(pictured right)*. It is made of a lightweight, rocky material and is covered with a layer of dust. Its largest crater, Voltaire, is 1.25 miles (2 km) across.

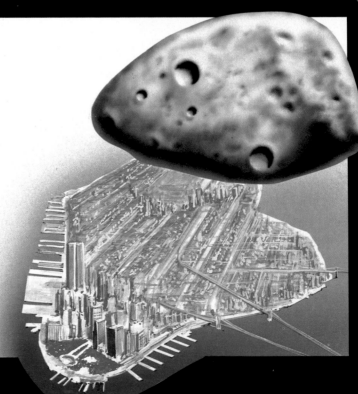

Callisto, another of Jupiter's moons, is 2,995 miles (4,820 km) across. For its size, it has more craters than any other planet or moon in the Solar System. The largest crater, Valhalla, is 373 miles (600 km) in diameter (about the size of Poland) and is surrounded by ripples about 1,864 miles (3,000 km) across.

THE LARGEST MOONS
WORLDS OF ICE AND ROCK

MOONS, sometimes known as **satellites**, are small bodies that circle the planets of the Solar System. Earth has one moon, known simply as the Moon, but the larger planets have many more. Saturn has at least eighteen moons. Moons are as varied in size and form as the planets themselves. Astronomers say there are two ways in which moons come into being. Some form as the result of fragments of rock and ice coming together to make a globe. Others are **asteroids** that have been captured by a planet's force of gravity *(see page 10).* All seven largest moons illustrated here are larger than the smallest planet, Pluto. Mercury, the second smallest planet (with a diameter approximately the same as the distance across Canada and Alaska) is smaller than both Ganymede and Titan.

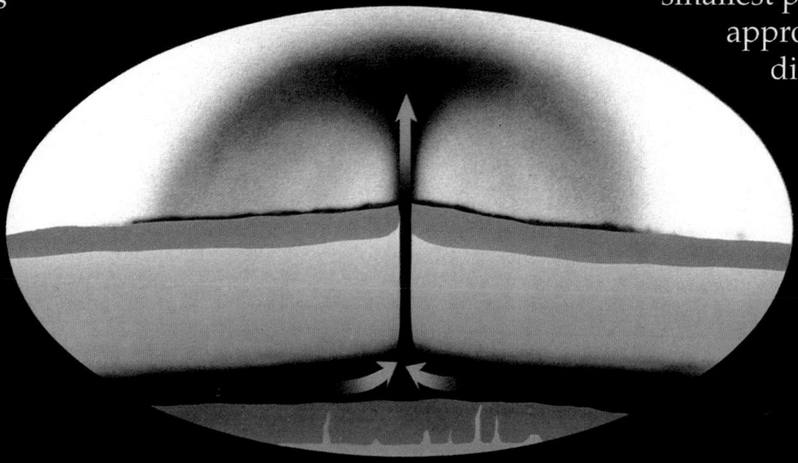

CALLISTO

Io's volcanoes *(above)* erupt liquid sulfur in plumes that reach heights of 174 miles (280 km). The ejected matter is blasted out at 2,237 miles (3,600 km) per hour.

Europa, Jupiter's fourth largest moon, is 1,943 miles (3,126 km) across. Europa is the smoothest body in the Solar System. The largest hills on its icy crust measure only about 984 feet (300 m) high.

Triton, Neptune's largest moon, is 1,690 miles (2,720 km) across. Triton's surface is the coldest place in the Solar System. Its temperature of -391°F (-235°C) is low enough to freeze oxygen and nitrogen.

IO

Io, Jupiter's third largest moon, is 2,257 miles (3,632 km) across. For its size, it is the most volcanically active body in the Solar System. At any one time, there are seven or eight eruptions in progress. Only Earth has more active volcanoes.

MOON

Our own Moon, Earth's nearest neighbor in space, is 2,160 miles (3,476 km) across, the fifth largest moon in the Solar System. It would take eighty-one Moons to equal the size of Earth.

EUROPA

TRITON

HALLEY'S COMET

THE BRIGHTEST SHORT-PERIOD COMET

T HE MOST FAMOUS of all comets is named after the English astronomer Edmund Halley (1656-1742). He was the first to predict that this comet would return to the night skies every 75-76 years.

Halley believed that comets, like the planets, travel around the Sun in **elliptical** orbits. He examined the records of comets that had appeared in 1531 and 1607. Then he suggested that they, along with a comet he observed in 1682, were, in fact, one and the same. On each occasion, people saw it passing close to Earth on its never-ending journey around the Sun. Halley did not live to see his theory come true. What is now known as Halley's Comet was next sighted on Christmas Day, 1758, seventy-five years after the astronomer had seen it.

Thousands of comets have been discovered. Those that complete their orbits in less than two hundred years are called short-period comets. Halley's Comet is the brightest of these. The long-period comets (over two hundred years) are often more spectacular, with longer tails. The record for the longest tail, measured at 199 million miles (320 million km), is held by the Great Comet of 1843.

A COMETARY JOURNEY

Halley's orbit takes it from just outside Neptune's orbit to just within that of Venus. As it approaches the Sun, it heats up, brightens, and grows a spectacular tail of gas and dust, always pointing away from the Sun. The comet travels away from the Sun, tail first. Eventually, it fades and its tail disappears — until the next time it nears the Sun.

Halley's Comet last approached Earth in 1986, but that year it was far away and barely visible. A remote-controlled spacecraft called *Giotto* did, however, successfully photograph it at close range. Halley's next visit will be in the year 2062.

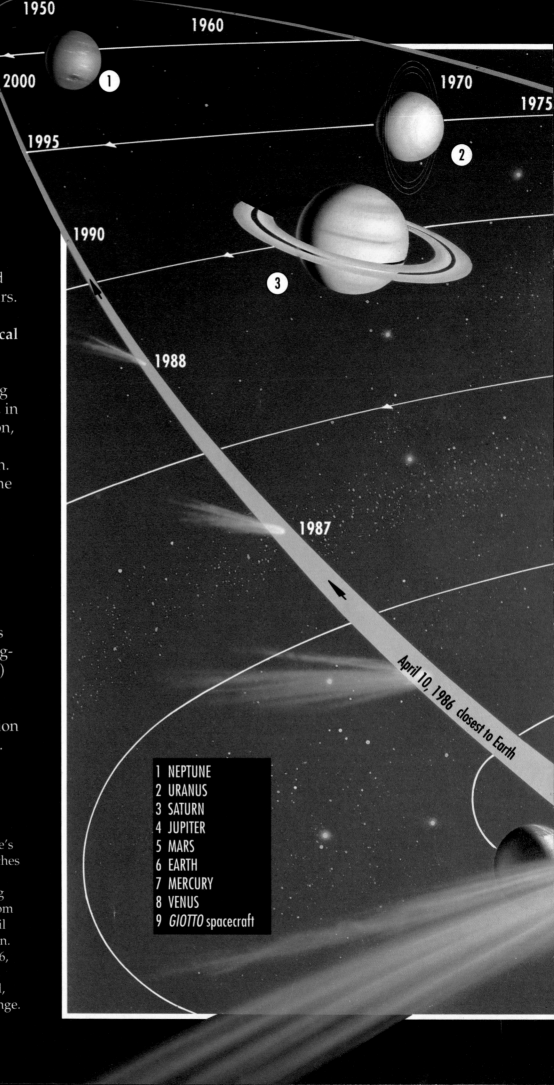

1 NEPTUNE
2 URANUS
3 SATURN
4 JUPITER
5 MARS
6 EARTH
7 MERCURY
8 VENUS
9 *GIOTTO* spacecraft

April 10, 1986 closest to Earth

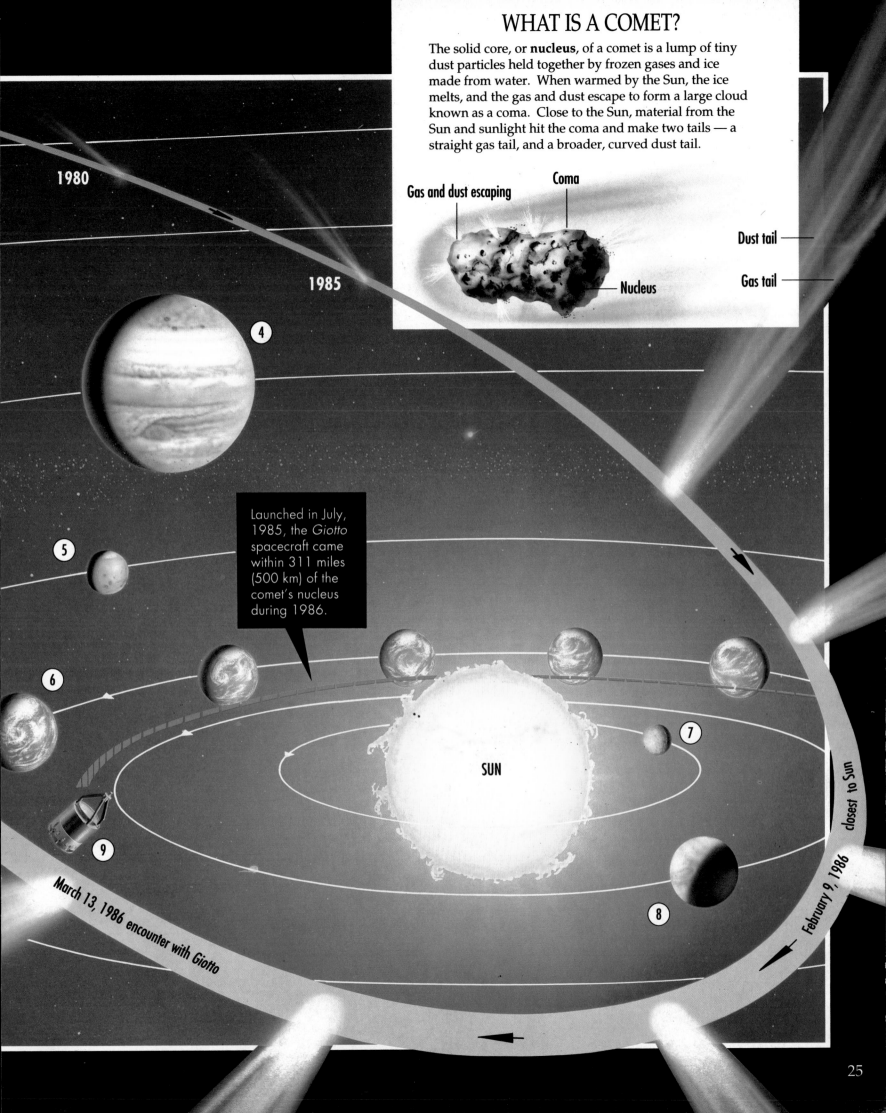

WHAT IS A COMET?

The solid core, or **nucleus**, of a comet is a lump of tiny dust particles held together by frozen gases and ice made from water. When warmed by the Sun, the ice melts, and the gas and dust escape to form a large cloud known as a coma. Close to the Sun, material from the Sun and sunlight hit the coma and make two tails — a straight gas tail, and a broader, curved dust tail.

Gas and dust escaping

Coma

Dust tail

Gas tail

Nucleus

1980

1985

Launched in July, 1985, the *Giotto* spacecraft came within 311 miles (500 km) of the comet's nucleus during 1986.

SUN

February 9, 1986 closest to Sun

March 13, 1986 encounter with Giotto

EARTH RECORD HOLDERS
OUR HOME PLANET

OF ALL THE PLANETS in our Solar System, Earth has the most water. Its atmosphere also contains the most oxygen. Without water, life could not have developed, and without plant life there would be no oxygen in the atmosphere. Without oxygen to breathe, no animals could exist.

The oceans occupy nearly three-quarters of Earth's surface. The largest ocean, the Pacific, accounts for half that area. More than one tenth of the land area is covered by permanent ice, mainly in the Antarctic and Greenland icecaps. About a third of the land surface forms the continent of Eurasia (Europe and Asia), the largest landmass.

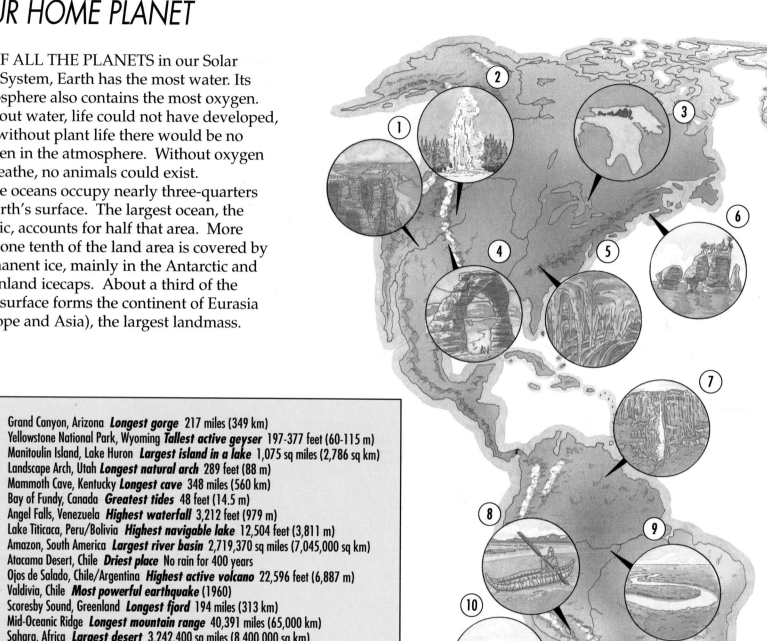

1	Grand Canyon, Arizona	**Longest gorge** 217 miles (349 km)
2	Yellowstone National Park, Wyoming	**Tallest active geyser** 197-377 feet (60-115 m)
3	Manitoulin Island, Lake Huron	**Largest island in a lake** 1,075 sq miles (2,786 sq km)
4	Landscape Arch, Utah	**Longest natural arch** 289 feet (88 m)
5	Mammoth Cave, Kentucky	**Longest cave** 348 miles (560 km)
6	Bay of Fundy, Canada	**Greatest tides** 48 feet (14.5 m)
7	Angel Falls, Venezuela	**Highest waterfall** 3,212 feet (979 m)
8	Lake Titicaca, Peru/Bolivia	**Highest navigable lake** 12,504 feet (3,811 m)
9	Amazon, South America	**Largest river basin** 2,719,370 sq miles (7,045,000 sq km)
10	Atacama Desert, Chile	**Driest place** No rain for 400 years
11	Ojos de Salado, Chile/Argentina	**Highest active volcano** 22,596 feet (6,887 m)
12	Valdivia, Chile	**Most powerful earthquake** (1960)
13	Scoresby Sound, Greenland	**Longest fjord** 194 miles (313 km)
14	Mid-Oceanic Ridge	**Longest mountain range** 40,391 miles (65,000 km)
15	Sahara, Africa	**Largest desert** 3,242,400 sq miles (8,400,000 sq km)
16	Al'Aziziyah, Libya	**Hottest place** Highest temperature 136.4°F (58°C)
17	Nile, Africa	**Longest river** 4,145 miles (6,670 km)
18	Great Rift Valley	**Greatest rift valley** 3,977 miles (6,400 km)
19	Pripet Marshes, Belarus	**Largest swamp** 18,123 sq miles (46,950 sq km)
20	Caspian Sea	**Largest lake** 143,206 sq miles (371,000 sq km)
21	Dead Sea, Israel/Jordan	**Lowest point on land** 1,312 feet (400 m) below sea level
22	Lake Baikal, Russia	**Deepest lake** 5,371 feet (1,637 m)
23	Tibet	**Highest plateau** 15,995 feet (4,875 m)
24	Cherrapunji, India	**Wettest place** 1,043 inches (26,461 millimeters) rain in a year-1861
25	Mount Everest, Nepal/Tibet	**Highest mountain** 29,080 feet (8,863 m)
26	Ganges/Brahmaputra, India/Bangladesh	**Largest delta** 28,950 sq feet (75,000 sq km)
27	Marianas Trench	**Deepest point on Earth** 36,196 feet (11,032 m)
28	Indonesia	**Largest archipelago** More than 13,000 islands
29	Tambora, Indonesia	**Greatest volcanic eruption** (1815)
30	Uluru (Ayers Rock), Australia	**Largest fully exposed monolith** 1,142 feet (348 m) high; 1.9 miles (3.1 km) long
31	Great Barrier Reef, Australia	**Longest coral reef** 1,260 miles (2,027 km)
32	Pole of Cold, Antarctica	**Coldest place** Average temperature -72°F (-57.8°C)

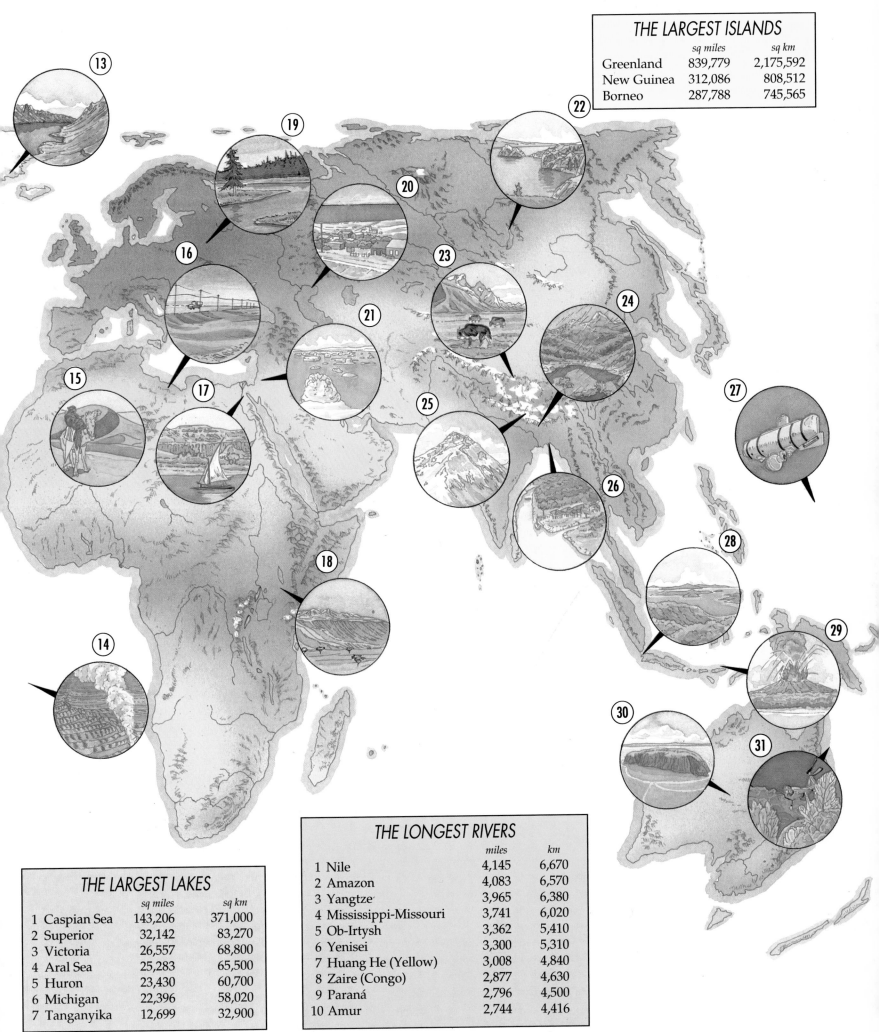

THE LARGEST ISLANDS

	sq miles	sq km
Greenland	839,779	2,175,592
New Guinea	312,086	808,512
Borneo	287,788	745,565

THE LONGEST RIVERS

		miles	km
1	Nile	4,145	6,670
2	Amazon	4,083	6,570
3	Yangtze	3,965	6,380
4	Mississippi-Missouri	3,741	6,020
5	Ob-Irtysh	3,362	5,410
6	Yenisei	3,300	5,310
7	Huang He (Yellow)	3,008	4,840
8	Zaire (Congo)	2,877	4,630
9	Paraná	2,796	4,500
10	Amur	2,744	4,416

THE LARGEST LAKES

		sq miles	sq km
1	Caspian Sea	143,206	371,000
2	Superior	32,142	83,270
3	Victoria	26,557	68,800
4	Aral Sea	25,283	65,500
5	Huron	23,430	60,700
6	Michigan	22,396	58,020
7	Tanganyika	12,699	32,900

THE GREATEST OCEAN
THE MIGHTY PACIFIC

The Pacific Ocean has deep trenches, vast seafloor plains peppered with volcanoes, and steep continental slopes.

The deepest part of the ocean floor in the world is a plain east of Japan (2). This area has an average depth of 14,994 feet (4,570 m).

②

Earth's deepest point, the Marianas Trench (1).

①

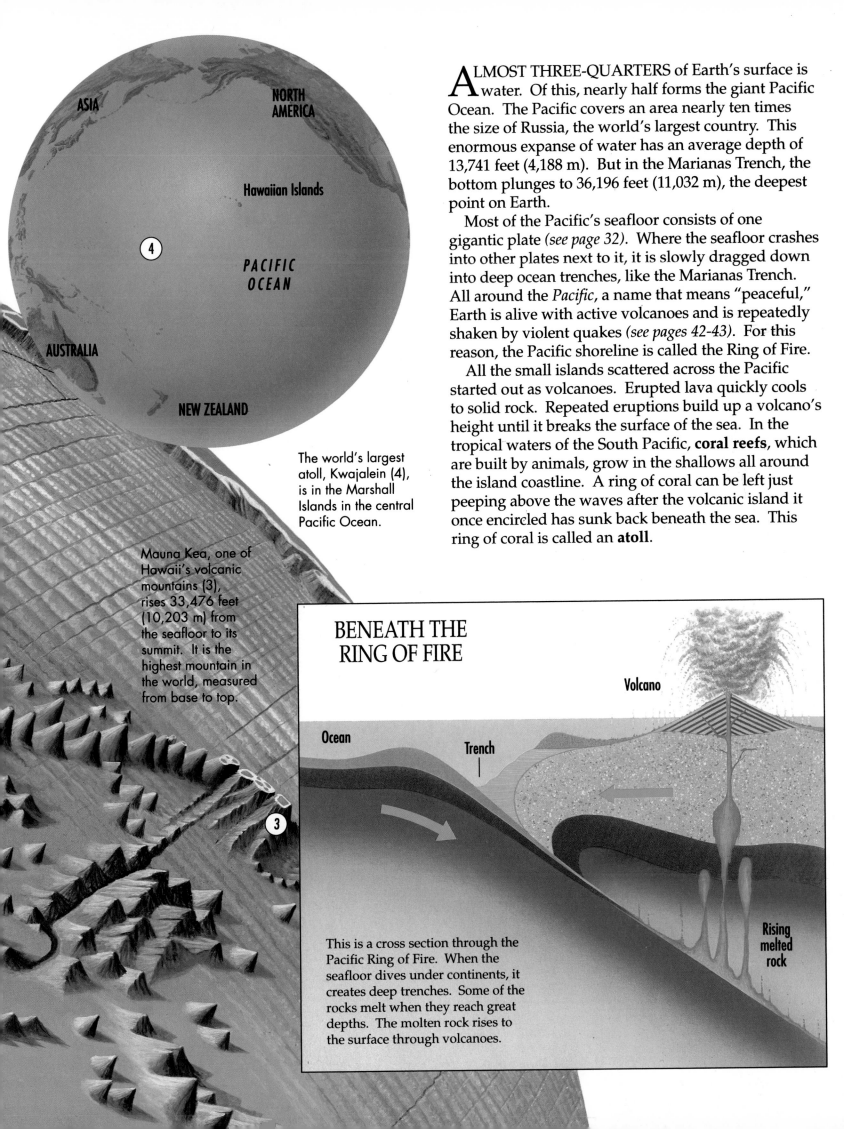

ALMOST THREE-QUARTERS of Earth's surface is water. Of this, nearly half forms the giant Pacific Ocean. The Pacific covers an area nearly ten times the size of Russia, the world's largest country. This enormous expanse of water has an average depth of 13,741 feet (4,188 m). But in the Marianas Trench, the bottom plunges to 36,196 feet (11,032 m), the deepest point on Earth.

Most of the Pacific's seafloor consists of one gigantic plate (see page 32). Where the seafloor crashes into other plates next to it, it is slowly dragged down into deep ocean trenches, like the Marianas Trench. All around the *Pacific*, a name that means "peaceful," Earth is alive with active volcanoes and is repeatedly shaken by violent quakes (see pages 42-43). For this reason, the Pacific shoreline is called the Ring of Fire.

All the small islands scattered across the Pacific started out as volcanoes. Erupted lava quickly cools to solid rock. Repeated eruptions build up a volcano's height until it breaks the surface of the sea. In the tropical waters of the South Pacific, **coral reefs**, which are built by animals, grow in the shallows all around the island coastline. A ring of coral can be left just peeping above the waves after the volcanic island it once encircled has sunk back beneath the sea. This ring of coral is called an **atoll**.

ASIA

NORTH AMERICA

Hawaiian Islands

4

PACIFIC OCEAN

AUSTRALIA

NEW ZEALAND

The world's largest atoll, Kwajalein (4), is in the Marshall Islands in the central Pacific Ocean.

Mauna Kea, one of Hawaii's volcanic mountains (3), rises 33,476 feet (10,203 m) from the seafloor to its summit. It is the highest mountain in the world, measured from base to top.

3

BENEATH THE RING OF FIRE

Volcano

Ocean

Trench

Rising melted rock

This is a cross section through the Pacific Ring of Fire. When the seafloor dives under continents, it creates deep trenches. Some of the rocks melt when they reach great depths. The molten rock rises to the surface through volcanoes.

THE GREATEST MOUNTAIN RANGE
THE MID-OCEANIC RIDGE

HIDDEN BENEATH THE OCEANS is the world's greatest mountain range. Called the Mid-Oceanic Ridge, it starts in the Arctic Ocean and runs southward through the Atlantic before bending to the east, winding through the Indian and Pacific oceans. It ends up near the west coast of North America after a journey of 40,391 miles (65,000 km). Some of its peaks are 13,780 feet (4,200 m) high, but only a few break the ocean waters as tiny islands. Iceland has grown into a large island as volcanoes have erupted over and over again in the same place.

Beneath the Ridge, liquid rock or **magma** from the hot interior of Earth rises toward the surface. The seafloor bulges upward and cracks open. The magma, called lava as it bubbles out of Earth's crust, seeps into **faults** and pushes the rocks farther apart. Every year, the faults running down the Ridge grow wider — about the speed that fingernails grow. Over millions of years, the ocean floor itself becomes wider and wider.

There are much longer faults cutting across the Ridge at right-angles. These break up the seafloor into giant blocks, giving the Ridge a zigzag shape.

VOLCANOES UNDER THE SEA

Unlike the violent explosions of volcanoes like Santorini (*see pages 40-41*), eruptions along the Mid-Oceanic Ridge are fairly gentle. This is because the liquid rock flows easily. Along the center of the Ridge runs a rift valley, a strip of land between two parallel faults (*see pages 34-35*). Most of the eruptions happen here, where lava rises through the faults. Sometimes a volcano may erupt long enough to grow and reach the surface, where it forms an island in the ocean. Bouvet Island in the south Atlantic Ocean, the most remote island in the world — 1,056 miles (1,700 km) from the nearest land — arose in this way.

Deep in the central valley that runs the length of the Mid-Oceanic Ridge, tall "chimneys" made of solidified minerals, known as black smokers, blast hot smoke into the ocean waters. These black smokers provide warmth and food for certain crabs, worms, and fishes that are found nowhere else on Earth.

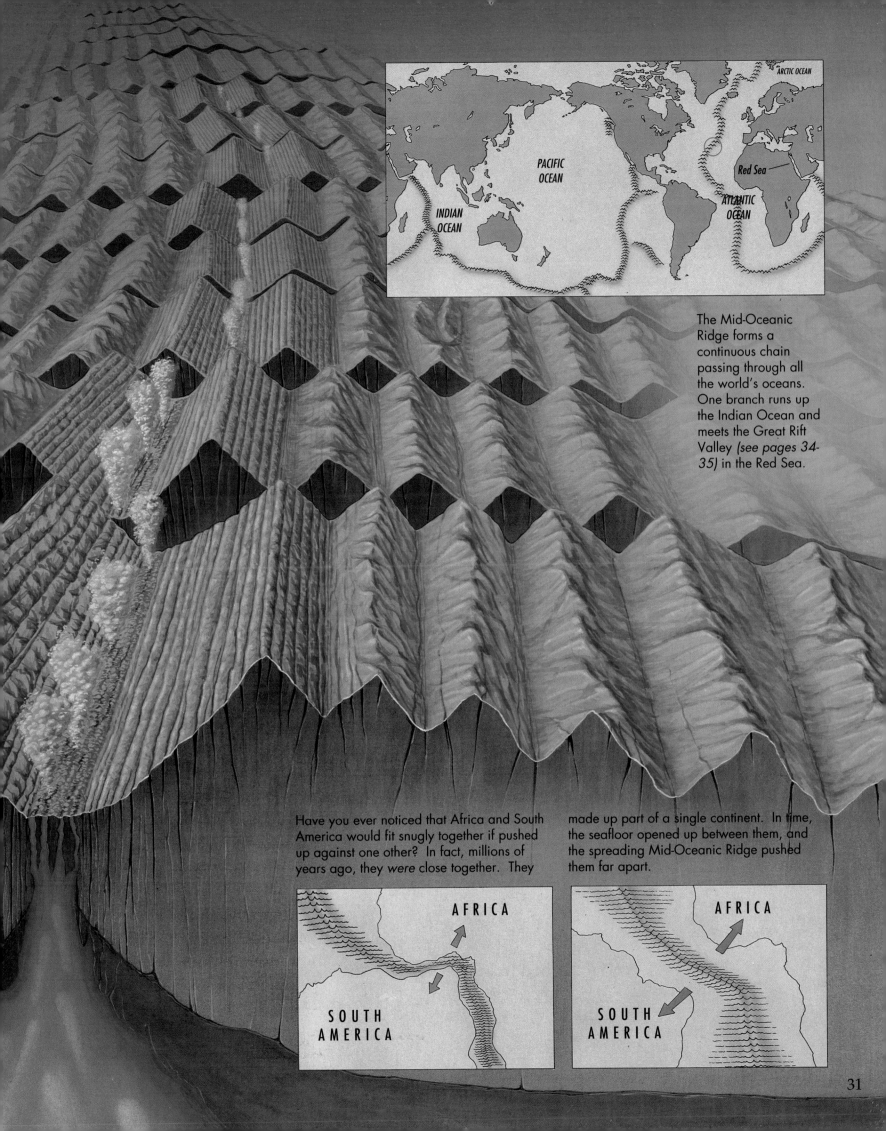

ARCTIC OCEAN

PACIFIC
OCEAN

INDIAN
OCEAN

Red Sea

ATLANTIC
OCEAN

The Mid-Oceanic Ridge forms a continuous chain passing through all the world's oceans. One branch runs up the Indian Ocean and meets the Great Rift Valley *(see pages 34-35)* in the Red Sea.

Have you ever noticed that Africa and South America would fit snugly together if pushed up against one other? In fact, millions of years ago, they *were* close together. They made up part of a single continent. In time, the seafloor opened up between them, and the spreading Mid-Oceanic Ridge pushed them far apart.

AFRICA

SOUTH
AMERICA

AFRICA

SOUTH
AMERICA

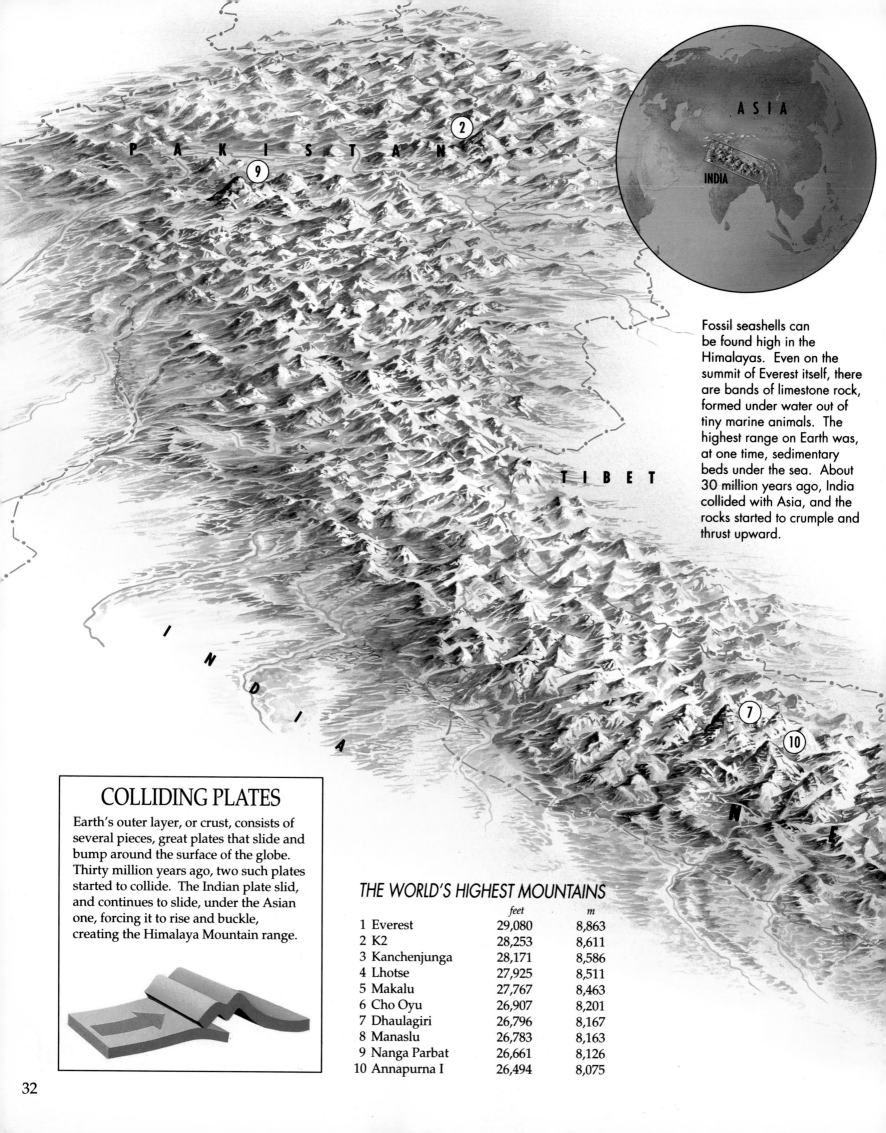

ASIA

INDIA

P A K I S T A N

②

⑨

T I B E T

I N D I A

⑦

⑩

N

E

Fossil seashells can be found high in the Himalayas. Even on the summit of Everest itself, there are bands of limestone rock, formed under water out of tiny marine animals. The highest range on Earth was, at one time, sedimentary beds under the sea. About 30 million years ago, India collided with Asia, and the rocks started to crumple and thrust upward.

COLLIDING PLATES

Earth's outer layer, or crust, consists of several pieces, great plates that slide and bump around the surface of the globe. Thirty million years ago, two such plates started to collide. The Indian plate slid, and continues to slide, under the Asian one, forcing it to rise and buckle, creating the Himalaya Mountain range.

THE WORLD'S HIGHEST MOUNTAINS

		feet	*m*
1	Everest	29,080	8,863
2	K2	28,253	8,611
3	Kanchenjunga	28,171	8,586
4	Lhotse	27,925	8,511
5	Makalu	27,767	8,463
6	Cho Oyu	26,907	8,201
7	Dhaulagiri	26,796	8,167
8	Manaslu	26,783	8,163
9	Nanga Parbat	26,661	8,126
10	Annapurna I	26,494	8,075

THE HIGHEST MOUNTAINS
THE TOWERING HIMALAYAS

THE HIMALAYA-KARAKORAM range is the greatest continental mountain range on Earth. It divides China in the north from Pakistan and India in the south. Nepal and Bhutan lie entirely within the Himalayas. The top ten summits, as well as about 90 per cent of the world's one hundred highest peaks, are found here. The highest peak of all (measured from sea level) is Mount Everest, which lies on the Tibet-Nepal border.

The Himalayas are still getting higher, as the forces that built the mountain chain *(see panel, below left)* continue to grind on. Tibet, to the north, the world's highest and largest plateau with an average height of 15,995 feet (4,875 m), was pushed up by the same processes. One day, millions of years into the future, another peak may perhaps take Everest's place as the world's highest.

As the mountains grow, they are attacked by wind, rain, frost, and ice. These forces of **erosion** produce the sharp, jagged peaks that make mountain scenery so spectacular. Eventually, these peaks will be worn down to become low, rounded hills.

The Himalayan glaciers and rivers have cut the world's deepest gorges, those of the Kali Gandak (between Annapurna and Dhaulagiri) and the Arun (east of Everest). Both plunge more than 3 miles (5 km) below neighboring summits.

The Everest and Lhotse peaks, first and fourth highest above sea level, form part of the same mountain mass. In the illustration *at right*, Everest is in the left foreground, Lhotse is to the right.

Given an additional name in honor of Colonel Sir George Everest (1790-1866), Surveyor-General of India, Mt. Everest is known to the Tibetans as Qomolangma and to the Nepalese as Sagarmatha.

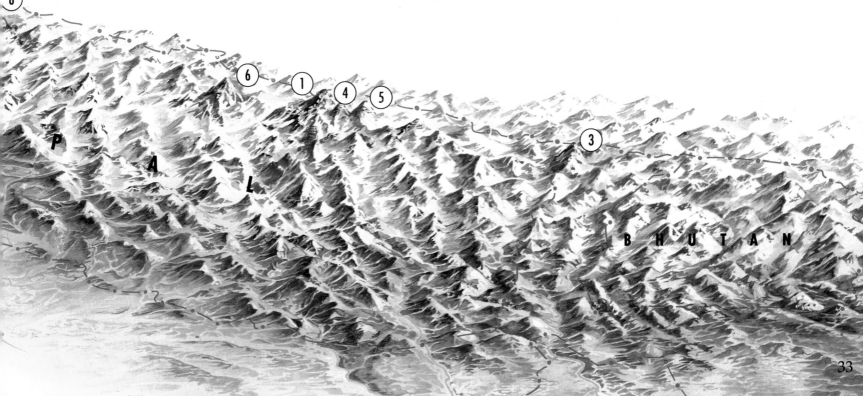

THE GREATEST RIFT
AND THE LONGEST RIVER

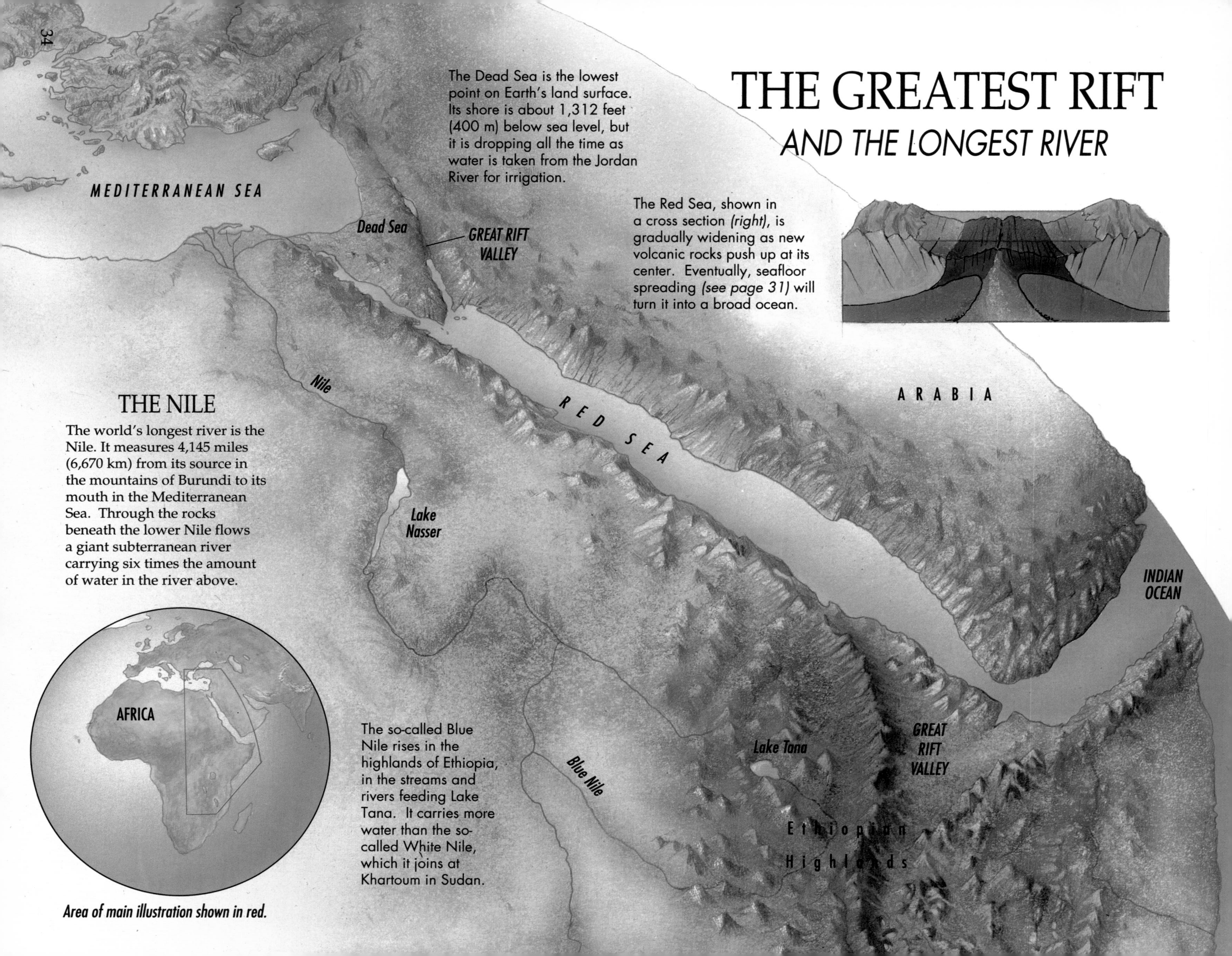

The Dead Sea is the lowest point on Earth's land surface. Its shore is about 1,312 feet (400 m) below sea level, but it is dropping all the time as water is taken from the Jordan River for irrigation.

The Red Sea, shown in a cross section (right), is gradually widening as new volcanic rocks push up at its center. Eventually, seafloor spreading (see page 31) will turn it into a broad ocean.

GREAT RIFT VALLEY

Dead Sea

MEDITERRANEAN SEA

Nile

Lake Nasser

THE NILE

The world's longest river is the Nile. It measures 4,145 miles (6,670 km) from its source in the mountains of Burundi to its mouth in the Mediterranean Sea. Through the rocks beneath the lower Nile flows a giant subterranean river carrying six times the amount of water in the river above.

The so-called Blue Nile rises in the highlands of Ethiopia, in the streams and rivers feeding Lake Tana. It carries more water than the so-called White Nile, which it joins at Khartoum in Sudan.

INDIAN OCEAN

ARABIA

RED SEA

GREAT RIFT VALLEY

Ethiopian Highlands

Lake Tana

Blue Nile

AFRICA

Area of main illustration shown in red.

Lake Turkana

GREAT RIFT VALLEY

Kilimanjaro

Lake Malawi

Lake Victoria

Source of the Nile

GREAT RIFT VALLEY

Lake Tanganyika

White Nile

This is a view of the Great Rift Valley in East Africa (above). It was here, scientists believe, that our human ancestors first appeared.

EAST AFRICA SPLITS APART

THE GREAT RIFT VALLEY cuts a path through East Africa. Two branches of the valley run northward on either side of Lake Victoria. They meet, and the valley runs on through Ethiopia, the Red Sea, and the Dead Sea, finally ending up in southern Syria. The greatest cleft in Earth's surface above sea level, the Great Rift Valley runs 3,977 miles (6,400 km). Only the rift in the Mid-Oceanic Ridge is longer (see pages 30-31).

Land, hundreds of miles wide in some places, has dropped down between gigantic faults in Earth's crust. On each side, high cliffs tower above the valley floor. Volcanoes spew lava that has forced its way up from deep inside Earth (see pages 40-41). One day, an arm of the Indian Ocean might fill the valley, turning East Africa into an island. This has already happened in a stretch of the valley to the north, now lying beneath the Red Sea.

The source of the White Nile (the longest branch) lies south of the Equator in Burundi. It lies in mountains bordering Lake Tanganyika, the world's second deepest lake. Its greatest depth is 4,823 feet (1,470 m). From there, it flows into and out of Lake Victoria on its long journey to the coast.

35

THE LARGEST GORGE
THE SPECTACULAR GRAND CANYON

THE GRAND CANYON in Arizona is the largest gorge on Earth. It twists and turns across dry, rocky land for 217 miles (349 km). Averaging 9.9 miles (16 km) in width and 1 mile (1.6 km) in depth, this vast chasm has been carved by the savage force of the Colorado River and its tributaries. And the process continues today. On a normal day, the river carries off about 0.55 million tons (0.5 million metric tons) of sediment. When the river floods, large boulders are swept downstream.

The Colorado River has been changing the land for millions of years, cutting downward as the land beneath it has gradually risen higher and higher. Over a period of about five million years, the land has increased in height by more than 3,937 feet (1,200 m). In the meantime, the Colorado has carved through to rocks buried deep below the ground that once formed the lower slopes of ancient mountains standing 52,496 feet (16,000 m) high — twice that of Mount Everest.

An aerial view *(below)* of the Grand Canyon in Arizona.

A cross section through the Grand Canyon shows the various layers of rock.

Colorado River

HISTORY IN THE ROCKS

Nearly a complete display of Earth's history is revealed on the slopes of the Grand Canyon. As the land lay under the sea for hundreds of millions of years, layers of sediment were laid down, one layer on top of the other. Each layer turned to stone, the different types reflecting the climates and life-forms of their age. The oldest rocks in the Grand Canyon, found in the deepest part of the gorge, are 1.7 billion years old.

Colorado River

USA

① ② ③

The Colorado River once flowed gently across the desert (1). Then, between 10 and 12 million years ago, the land beneath it began to rise (2). It did so only by about 0.01 inch (0.25 mm) a year. But the river kept pace with it, cutting a deeper channel to preserve its downward course to the sea. It carved through various layers of rock, some hard, some soft. The soft layers wore away more easily. Today, they stand as vertical cliff faces (3).

This is a bird's-eye view of the Grand Canyon, showing the arid terrain and characteristic step-like slopes. The Grand Canyon exists only because the climate of the region has always been extremely dry. (The Colorado River's water comes from the distant Rockies.) If there had been more rainfall, most of the soft, upper layers of rock would have been washed away.

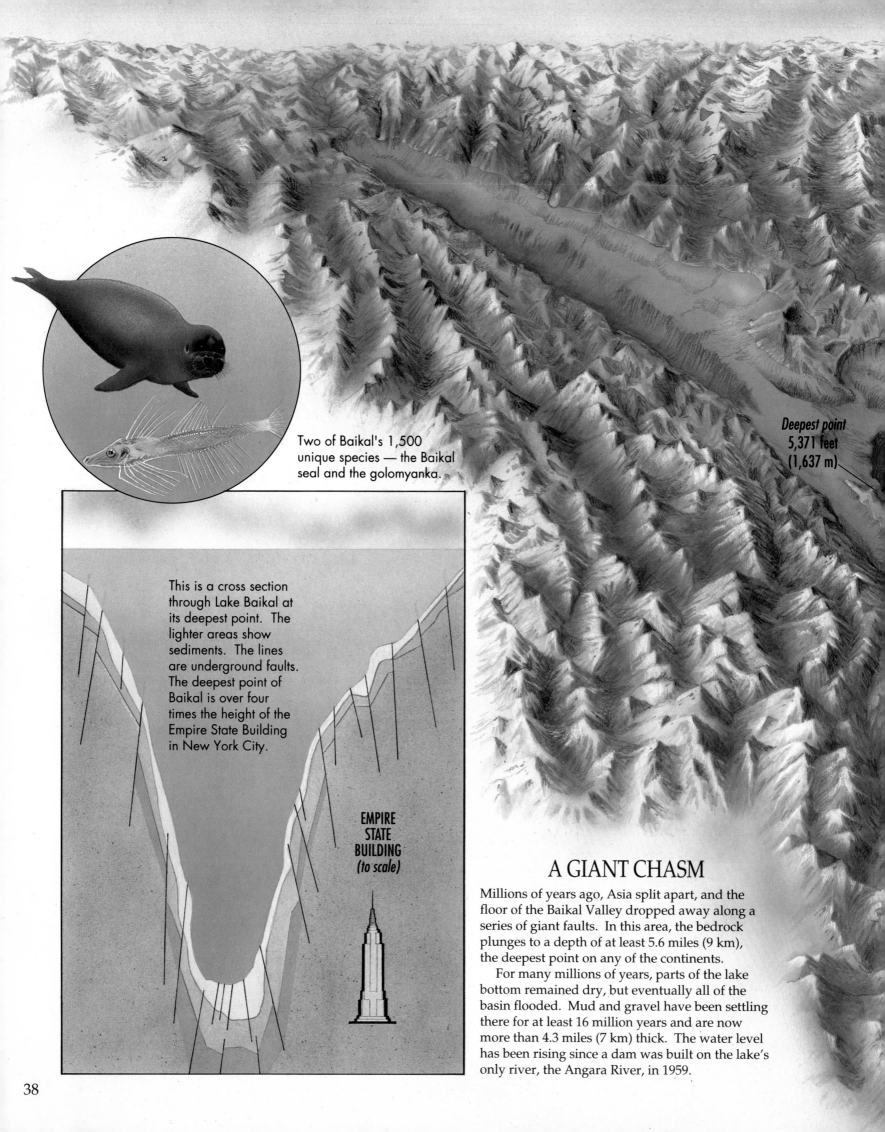

Two of Baikal's 1,500 unique species — the Baikal seal and the golomyanka.

This is a cross section through Lake Baikal at its deepest point. The lighter areas show sediments. The lines are underground faults. The deepest point of Baikal is over four times the height of the Empire State Building in New York City.

EMPIRE STATE BUILDING
(to scale)

Deepest point
5,371 feet
(1,637 m)

A GIANT CHASM

Millions of years ago, Asia split apart, and the floor of the Baikal Valley dropped away along a series of giant faults. In this area, the bedrock plunges to a depth of at least 5.6 miles (9 km), the deepest point on any of the continents.

For many millions of years, parts of the lake bottom remained dry, but eventually all of the basin flooded. Mud and gravel have been settling there for at least 16 million years and are now more than 4.3 miles (7 km) thick. The water level has been rising since a dam was built on the lake's only river, the Angara River, in 1959.

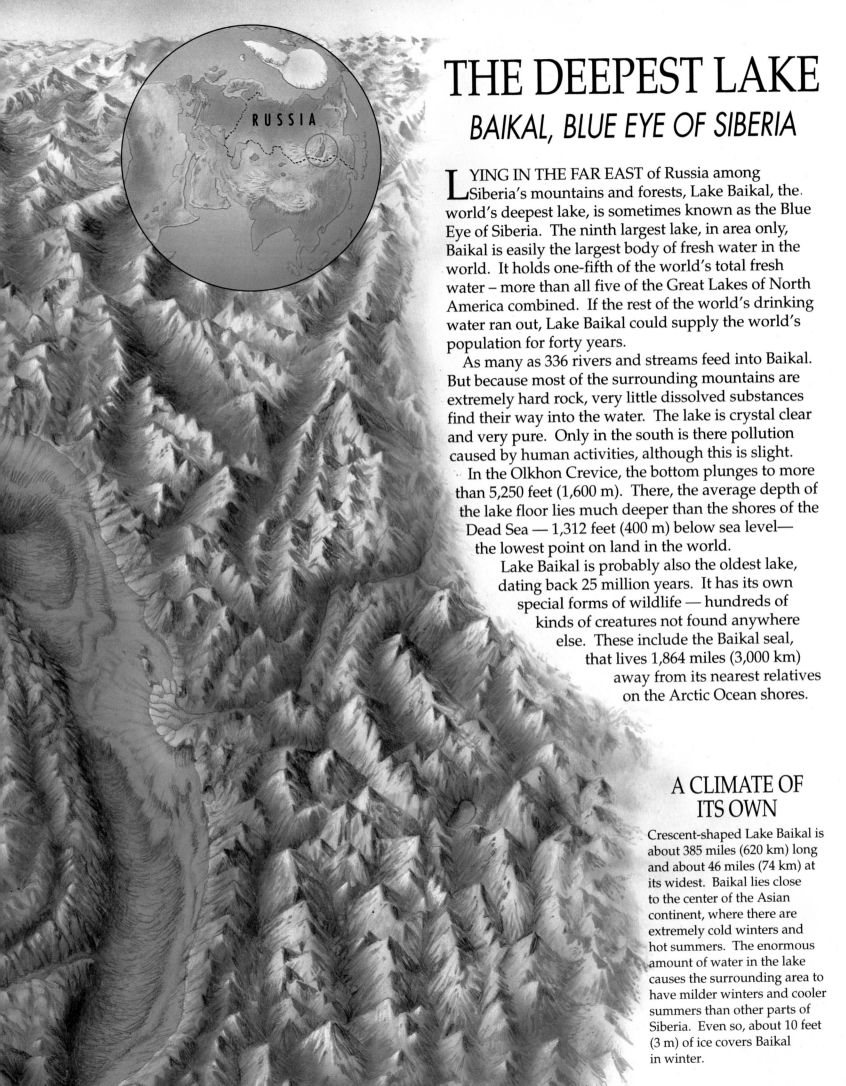

THE DEEPEST LAKE
BAIKAL, BLUE EYE OF SIBERIA

RUSSIA

LYING IN THE FAR EAST of Russia among Siberia's mountains and forests, Lake Baikal, the world's deepest lake, is sometimes known as the Blue Eye of Siberia. The ninth largest lake, in area only, Baikal is easily the largest body of fresh water in the world. It holds one-fifth of the world's total fresh water – more than all five of the Great Lakes of North America combined. If the rest of the world's drinking water ran out, Lake Baikal could supply the world's population for forty years.

As many as 336 rivers and streams feed into Baikal. But because most of the surrounding mountains are extremely hard rock, very little dissolved substances find their way into the water. The lake is crystal clear and very pure. Only in the south is there pollution caused by human activities, although this is slight.

In the Olkhon Crevice, the bottom plunges to more than 5,250 feet (1,600 m). There, the average depth of the lake floor lies much deeper than the shores of the Dead Sea — 1,312 feet (400 m) below sea level— the lowest point on land in the world.

Lake Baikal is probably also the oldest lake, dating back 25 million years. It has its own special forms of wildlife — hundreds of kinds of creatures not found anywhere else. These include the Baikal seal, that lives 1,864 miles (3,000 km) away from its nearest relatives on the Arctic Ocean shores.

A CLIMATE OF ITS OWN

Crescent-shaped Lake Baikal is about 385 miles (620 km) long and about 46 miles (74 km) at its widest. Baikal lies close to the center of the Asian continent, where there are extremely cold winters and hot summers. The enormous amount of water in the lake causes the surrounding area to have milder winters and cooler summers than other parts of Siberia. Even so, about 10 feet (3 m) of ice covers Baikal in winter.

When the Santorini volcano blew its top, violent gas explosions shot vast quantities of lava, ash, and dust high into the sky at the speed of sound (2). The entire mountaintop was destroyed in what was probably the greatest explosion of all time.

Santorini, today called Thera, was once a single Mediterranean island dominated by a **dormant** volcano about 5,250 feet (1,600 m) high (1). The land was fertile and occupied by the peaceful Minoan civilization centered on nearby Crete. At the port, there was a city. All this was to change in 1450 B.C. due to the volcanic eruption.

UNDER A VOLCANO

Volcanoes erupt gases and water as well as lava, ash, cinders, and dust.

Some volcanoes, like Kilauea on Hawaii, throw out lava that flows freely down the mountainside. They often erupt without great explosions. Other volcanoes have stiff, pasty lava that hardens quickly. Sometimes a plug of solid lava blocks the pathway to the surface. Pressure builds up in the magma chamber beneath the volcano until the plug is blasted away in a great explosion. Besides erupting streams of hot lava, volcanoes, such as Santorini, Vesuvius, and Krakatau, often shoot large quantities of cinders, ash, and dust high into the air.

The eruption went on for days. Soon, the ever-widening crater collapsed below sea level. Water flooded in (3), triggering even more gigantic explosions as the water washed over red-hot lava. Eventually, nearly all of the island of Santorini was blasted into the sky (4).

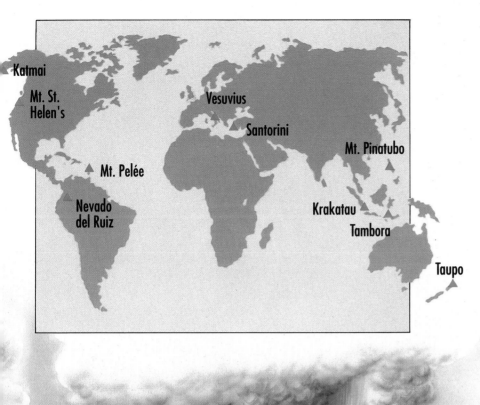

THE GREATEST EXPLOSION
A VOLCANO BLOWS

VOLCANIC ERUPTIONS, the most powerful explosions on Earth, are incredibly destructive. During the eruption of Krakatau in 1883, about 4.8 cubic miles (20 cu km) of rock, or nearly the entire mountain, was blasted high into the air. The noise of the explosion, the greatest of recent times, was heard over 3,107 miles (5,000 km) away in India, China, and Australia. But probably three times as much rock was ejected during the eruption of Santorini around 1450 B.C. Greater still was the eruption of Tambora on the island of Sumbawa in Indonesia in 1815, when about 38 cubic miles (160 cu km) of rock was blasted away. Pulverized rock was thrown 31 miles (50 km) high into Earth's atmosphere. Dust drifted around the globe, blocking the Sun's rays and causing temperatures to drop.

FAMOUS VOLCANIC ERUPTIONS OF THE PAST	
	Date
Santorini, Greece	1450 B.C.
Vesuvius, Italy	A.D. 79
Taupo, New Zealand	150
Tambora, Sumbawa	1815
Krakatau, Java	1883
Mount Pelée, Martinique	1902
Katmai, Alaska, USA	1912
Mt. St. Helen's, Washington, USA	1980
Nevado del Ruiz, Colombia	1985
Mt. Pinatubo, Philippines	1991

(Volcano sites on map, top left)

All that remains today is a ring of five small islands (5). One day, the volcanic islands in the center of the bay may grow into a large, new volcano.

This is a cross section of the region affected by the 1960 earthquake in Chile. Here, the Pacific Ocean floor is gradually plunging beneath the South American continent. A sudden jolt *(marked by the explosion on the illustration)* sent intense vibrations across a wide area and resulted in a devastating earthquake.

GIANT WAVES

Sudden movement of the seafloor during an earthquake creates waves that race across the oceans at about 435 miles (700 km) per hour. When the waves approach land, they rear up to 40 feet (12 m) or more *(above)*. Called **tsunamis**, they crash to shore, causing great destruction. In 1771, a tsunami off a Japanese island rose to 279 feet (85 m), or twenty-two stories high.

Most major earthquakes occur around the Ring of Fire *(the coastline of the Pacific Ocean, see page 29)*. Others happen in places where plates *(see page 32)* are pushing against one another — in central Asia and around the Mediterranean Sea.

PACIFIC OCEAN

Anchorage

Gansu Tangshan
San Francisco
Spitak
Lisbon
Assam
Tokyo
Mexico City
Messina
PACIFIC OCEAN
Guatemala

Valparaiso
Concepción
Valdivia

THE GREATEST EARTHQUAKE
THE GREAT CHILEAN QUAKE

ON MAY 22, 1960, a giant fault, 373 miles (600 km) long, deep beneath the ground in western South America, suddenly "slipped" about 66 feet (20 m). Then, a vast area of land in southern Chile was violently shaken for nearly four minutes. In the town of Valdivia, buildings were reduced to rubble. Part of the ocean floor dropped away, causing the sea to rush away from the shore, then return in several giant waves, 33 feet (10 m) high. The waves smashed into the shore and flung ships far inland. It was the most powerful earthquake ever recorded. A smaller tremor about ten minutes earlier had sent most people rushing into the streets. This saved many lives when the main quake came, although about 5,000 people did perish. Astonishingly, this is a small number when compared with the most deadly earthquake of recent times. A quake that occurred on July 28, 1976, killed about 750,000 people in Tangshan, China. The force of earthquakes is often described on the **Richter scale** — the larger the number, the worse the earthquake. The Chilean earthquake measured 9.5, and the Tangshan one, 7.8.

In the Chilean earthquake, over 400,000 houses were destroyed in minutes as the ground rocked beneath them. Giant cracks and holes opened in the surface of Earth, splitting the foundations of buildings. Afterward, the town of Valdivia and a vast area of the surrounding countryside had sunk by about 6.6 feet (2 m).

SOME GIANT EARTHQUAKES

	Year
Lisbon, Portugal	1755
Concepción, Chile	1835
Assam, India	1897
San Francisco, California	1906
Valparaiso, Chile	1906
Messina, Italy	1908
Gansu, China	1920
Tokyo, Japan	1923
Valdivia, Chile	1960
Anchorage, Alaska	1964
Guatemala	1976
Tangshan, China	1976
Mexico City, Mexico	1985
Spitak, Armenia	1988

THE MOST POWERFUL STORM

THE DEADLY TORNADO

THE ATMOSPHERE, the envelope of gases that surrounds Earth, sometimes becomes extremely violent. Hurricanes are destructive, circular storms with wind speeds reaching 186 miles (300 km) per hour.

Even more powerful are tornadoes. A tornado is a twisting column of air with wind speeds of more than 250 miles (400 km) per hour, the highest speeds on Earth. A tornado completely destroys everything in its relatively narrow path. Ordinary thunderstorms are also incredibly powerful. Every day around the world there are 44,000 thunderstorms. Every second, there are 100 lightning strikes, each with a force of 100 million volts or more. The amount of power generated daily by such storms would be enough to supply the entire United States twice over!

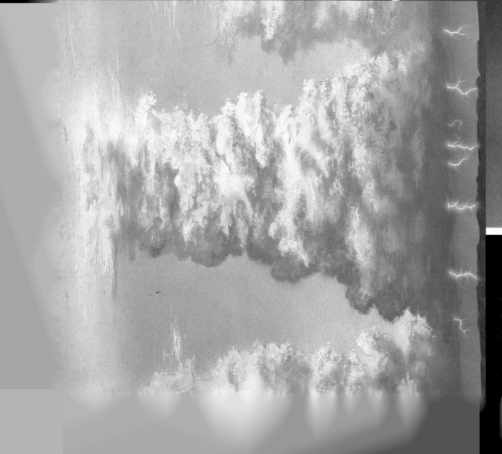

The tallest clouds are giant cumulonimbus clouds *(above)*. In the tropics, they may reach 12.5 miles (20 km) into the sky from their bases at 1,640 feet (500 m) above ground level. Air currents shoot up inside them at over 99 miles (160 km) per hour and can keep hailstones weighing as much as 1 pound (500 g) suspended in the air. Clusters of cumulonimbus clouds can produce thunderstorms, torrential rain, and tornadoes.

TRI-STATE TWISTER

Each year, the United States is hit by about a thousand tornadoes. The most devastating, the Tri-State Tornado, took shape on March 18, 1925. Traveling at about 62 miles (100 km) per hour, it lasted three-and-a-half hours and left a 218-mile (350-km) trail of destruction across the states of Missouri, Illinois, and Indiana (right). It killed 689 people, injured 1,980, destroyed 4 towns and made 11,000 people homeless. Eyewitnesses said it looked like a giant cone with lightning darting through it. It touched down with a thundering roar as though a freight train were speeding through.

BANGLADESH

In November, 1970, a cyclone hit the low-lying Ganges delta in Bangladesh (above). Violent winds and surging waves claimed the lives of up to half a million people. In terms of lives lost, it was the worst disaster caused by a storm in recorded history.

GLOSSARY

asteroid — a small planet that orbits the Sun, mainly in the region between Mars and Jupiter.

atmosphere — the gaseous layer that surrounds a planet. A layer of air surrounds Earth.

atoll — a coral reef that has grown around an island that is completely under water. A true atoll surrounds a blue lagoon.

black hole — a region in space that may be a collapsed star. It has a very strong gravitational pull.

constellation — a grouping of stars. The constellations are usually named after an outline of the animal, person, or object they resemble.

coral reef — a hardened collection of the skeletons of tiny sea animals.

corona — the circle around a luminous body in space, such as the Sun.

dormant — not active for a period of time.

eclipse — the blocking of the light from one body in space by another body in space.

elliptical — oval in shape; egg shaped.

erosion — the wearing away of an object by elements, such as water and the wind.

fault — a fracture or break in Earth's crust.

galaxy — a very large grouping of stars. Earth and our Sun are part of the Milky Way galaxy.

lava — the liquid rock that flows from an erupting volcano.

light-year — the distance light travels in one year, or about 5.9 trillion miles.

magma — liquified rock.

meteoroid — a fragment of rock and ice that orbits the Solar System.

nuclear fusion — a nuclear reaction in which two atomic nuclei combine to form a heavier nucleus, resulting in the release of energy.

nucleus — the central core of a structure.

photosphere — the surface of the Sun.

quasar — an object in space that resembles a star but is far more distant. It emits great amounts of light and radio waves.

radar — a scientific instrument that can locate objects and measure their speed.

Richter scale — a numerical scale that describes the force of earthquakes.

rift valley — a long valley formed by the falling of Earth's crust between two faults.

satellite — a body that orbits another, larger body in space, such as a planet. The Moon is Earth's natural satellite. Artificial satellites are launched from Earth by humans, usually for the study of outer space.

Solar System — the Sun, the nine planets, and the other bodies in space that orbit the Sun.

tsunami — a gigantic sea wave produced by an earthquake.

RESEARCH PROJECTS

1. At the library or on the Internet, research the latest information about the discovery of possible life-forms on Mars.

2. What are the various stages that a volcano goes through leading up to a violent eruption? What is the time frame of each stage? Are there scientific instruments that can detect an impending eruption so that people can be forewarned?

3. At the library or on the Internet, find out what types of scientific instruments are used to track violent weather.

4. Name the various types of clouds. What are the characteristics of each type? Which kinds have the potential to produce violent weather?

BOOKS

Colors of the Sea (series). Bearanger and Ethan (Gareth Stevens)

Earthquakes: A Natural History. Halacy (Macmillan)

Galaxies. Ferris (Stewart, Tabori, and Chang)

Himalayas. Majrani (Smithmark)

In Search of the Grand Canyon. Fraser (H. Holt)

Isaac Asimov's New Library of the Universe (series). Asimov (Gareth Stevens)

Planet Earth. Weiner (Bantam)

Planet Earth: Solar System. Frazier (Time-Life Books)

The Quest for Comets. D.H. Levy (Plenum Press)

The Satellite Atlas. Flint (Gareth Stevens)

The Sun. Simon (William Morrow)

True Adventures (series). Hurricane! The Rage of Hurricane Andrew. Lantier-Sampon (Gareth Stevens)

Universe. Kaufmann (W.H. Freeman)

The Universe and Life. Kutter (Jones and Bartlett)

Wonderworks of Nature (series). Storms: Nature's Fury. Volcanoes: Fire from Below. (Gareth Stevens)

The World Almanac. (World Almanac Books)

VIDEOS

Discovering Our Rivers, Lakes, and Oceans. (Film Ideas)

Earthquakes: Our Restless Planet. (Rainbow Educational Media)

Halley: A Comet Returns. (Encyclopædia Britannica Educational Corporation)

Hurricanes, Tornadoes, and Other Weather. (Journal Films and Video)

Isaac Asimov's New Library of the Universe (video series). (Gareth Stevens)

National Geographic: Volcano. (Columbia Tristar)

WEB SITES

www.fas.org/mars/

www.geo.mfu.edu/volcanoes/

bang.lanl.gov/solarsys/

www.tornadoproject.com/

www.leyada.jlm.k12.il/novell/black/plan.htm

PLACES TO VISIT

Edmonton Space and Science Centre
11211 - 142nd Street
Edmonton, Alberta T5M 4A1

American Museum of Natural History
Central Park West at 79th Street
New York, NY 10024

NASA Lyndon B. Johnson Space Center
2101 NASA Road One
Houston, TX 77058

International Women's Air and Space Museum
One Chamber Plaza
Dayton, OH 45402

The Space and Rocket Center and Space Camp
One Tranquility Base
Huntsville, AL 35807

Astrocentre Royal Ontario Museum
100 Queen's Park
Toronto, Ontario M5S 2C6

INDEX

A

Achernar 6-7
Al'Aziziyah (Libya) 26-27
Alpha Centauri 6-7
Altair 6
Amazon Basin 26
Amazon River 26-27
Angel Falls 26
Annapurna I 32
Antares 8
arch, longest natural 26
archipelago, largest 26-27
Arcturus 6
Arsia Mons 20
Arun gorge 33
Ascraeus Mons 20
asteroids 14-15, 23
Atacama Desert 26
atoll 29

B

Baikal, Lake 26-27, 38-39
Betelgeuse 6-7, 8
black holes 5, 9, 10-11
black smokers 30
Bouvet Island 30

C

Callisto 22-23
Canopus 6-7
canyons 26, 36-37
Capella 6
carbon dioxide 18, 21
Caspian Sea 26-27
cave, longest 26
Ceres 15
Charon 15
Cherrapunji 26-27
Cho Oyu 32-33
clouds 16-17, 18, 44
Colorado River 36-37
comets 16, 24-25
Concorde 7
constellations 6-7, 8
   largest 6-7
   smallest 6-7
coral reefs 26-27, 29
corona 13
craters 19, 22, 40
   most in Solar System 22
Crux 6-7
cumulonimbus 44
Cygnus X-1 11

D

Dead Sea 26-27, 34-35, 39
Deimos 22
delta, largest 26-27
desert, largest 26-27
Dhaulagiri 32
disaster, worst caused by a storm 45
dwarf stars 9

E

Earth
   coldest place 26
   crust 21
   deepest point 26-27, 28-29
   driest place 26
   highest points 26-27, 32-33
   hottest place 26-27
   largest landmass 26-27
   largest ocean 26
   lowest point on land 26-27, 34-35
   wettest place 26-27
earthquakes
   Chilean 42-43
   greatest-ever recorded 26, 42-43
   Tangshan 42-43
Eta Carinae 6-7
Europa 23
Everest, Mount 20, 26-27, 32-33, 36
explosion, greatest 30, 40-41

F

faults 30, 35, 38, 43
fjord, longest 26-27
flares, solar 12
Fundy, Bay of 26

G

galaxies 6-7, 9, 11
Galileo 22
Ganges delta 26-27, 45
Ganymede 22-23
gas giants 15
geyser, tallest active 26
Giotto spacecraft 24-25
gorges, largest and longest 21, 26, 33, 36-37
Grand Canyon 5, 21, 26, 36-37
gravity 8, 10-11, 16, 23
Great Barrier Reef 26-27
Great Red Spot 5, 16-17
Great Rift Valley 26-27, 30-31, 34-35
Greenland 26-27

H

Hadar 6-7
hailstones 44
Halley, Edmund 24
Halley's Comet 24-25
Hawaiian Islands 21, 40
helium 12, 15
Himalayas 20-21, 32-33
hot spot 20-21
hurricane 17, 44-45
Hydra 6-7
hydrogen 12, 15, 16-17

I

Iceland 30
Indonesia 26-27
Io 23
islands
   largest 27
   largest in a lake 26
   most remote 30

J

Japan 28, 42
Joint European Torus laboratory 12
Jupiter 5, 8, 12-13, 14-15, 16-17, 22-23, 24-25

K

K2 32
Kali Gandak gorge 33
Kanchenjunga 32-33
Karakoram 32-33
Katmai 41
Krakatau 40-41
Kwajalein Atoll 29

L

lakes
   deepest 26-27, 38-39
   highest navigable 26
   largest 26-27
   oldest 38-39
Landscape Arch 26
lava 21, 29, 30, 35, 40
Lhotse 32-33
light, speed of 7, 10
light-years 7
lightning 44-45

M

M31 galaxy 6
M33 galaxy 6
Magellan spacecraft 18-19
Magellanic Cloud, Large 6
magnetic fields 12
Makalu 32-33
Mammoth Cave 26
Manaslu 32-33

Manitoulin Island 26
Marianas Trench 26-27, 28-29
Mars 5, 8, 14-15, 20-21, 22, 24-25
Mauna Kea 29
Maxwell Montes 18
Mercury 8, 14-15, 18, 23, 24-25
meteoroids 19
Mid-Oceanic Ridge 26-27, 30-31, 35
Milky Way Galaxy 11
Moon 12, 13, 23
moons 14-15, 22-23
mountain ranges
   highest 20-21, 32-33
   longest 26-27, 30-31
mountains
   highest in Solar System 20-21
   highest on Earth 20-21, 26-27, 32-33
Mu Cephei 6, 8

N

Nanga Parbat 32
Neptune 15, 16, 23, 24
neutron stars 9, 10
Nevado del Ruiz 41
Nile, River 26-27, 34-35
Northern Hemisphere 6
nuclear fusion 12
nuclear reactions 8, 12

O

oceans 28-29, 30-31
   deepest area 28
   largest 26, 28-29
   trench 28-29
Ojos del Salado 26
Olympus Mons 18, 20-21
Orion 6-7, 8

P

Pacific Ocean 26, 28-29, 30, 42
Pavonis Mons 20
Pelée, Mount 41
photosphere 12
Pinatubo, Mount 41
planets 8, 10, 14-19, 21-26
   closest to Earth 14-15, 18-19
   closest to Sun 14-15
   coldest 15
   farthest from Sun 15
   first discovered by telescope 15
   hottest 14-15, 18-19
   largest 12-13, 14-15, 16-17
   largest rings 14-15
   most moons 14-15
   shortest day 14-15
   smallest 15
   smallest orbit around Sun 14-15
plateau, highest 26-27, 33
Pluto 5, 15, 23
Pole of Cold 26
Pripet Marshes 26-27
Procyon 6-7
prominences 12
protostars 8
Proxima Centauri 6-7

Q

Qomolangma 33
quasars 7, 10-11

R

Ras Algethi 8
red giant stars 9
Red Sea 34-35
Richter scale 43
rift valleys, greatest 21, 26-27, 30-31, 34-35
Rigel 6-7
Ring of Fire 29, 42
rivers
   largest basin 26-27
   longest 26-27, 34-35

S

Sagarmatha 33
Sagittarius Dwarf Galaxy 6-7
Sahara desert 26-27
sand dunes, largest area in Solar System 21
Santorini 30, 40-41
Saturn 5, 8, 14-15, 16, 22-23, 24
   moons 22-23
Scoresby Sound 26-27
Siberia 39
Sirius 6-7
solar eclipse 13
Solar System 5, 8, 12, 14-21, 22-23, 24-25, 26-27
   coldest place 23
   fastest winds 16
   highest mountain in 20-21
   hottest place 12
Southern Hemisphere 6-7
St. Helen's, Mt. 41
stars
   brightest 6-7
   largest 5, 6, 8-9
   life and death of 8-9
   most massive 6-7
   nearest 6-7, 12-13
   remains of 10-11
   smallest 9
storms, most powerful 44-45
Sun 8-9, 10, 12-13, 14-15, 16, 18, 21, 22, 24-25
   eclipse of 13
   sunspots 5, 12-13
      largest 5, 13
supergiant stars 8-9, 11
supernovas 9, 10
swamp, largest 26-27

T

Tambora 26-27, 41
Taupo 41
Tharsis Ridge 20
thunderstorms 44
Tibet 26-27, 32-33
tides, greatest 26
Titan 22-23
Titicaca, Lake 26
tornadoes 5, 44-45
Tri-State Tornado 45
Triton 23
tsunamis 42

U

Uluru 26-27
universe
   densest object in 10-11
   farthest visible object in 6
   most distant object in 11
Uranus 14-15, 16, 24

V

Valdivia 26, 42-43
Valhalla 22
Vallis Marineris 21
Vega 6
Venus 5, 8, 14-15, 18-19, 24-25
Vesuvius 40-41
volcanoes 18, 20-21, 23, 26-27, 28-29, 30, 34-35, 40-41
VV Cephei B 8

W

waterfall, highest 26
waves, highest 42
winds
   fastest in Solar System 5, 16
   fastest on Earth 5, 44